MW00773144

A
GUIDE TO CHRIST,

OR,

THE WAY OF DIRECTING SOULS
THAT ARE UNDER THE WORK OF
CONVERSION

COMPILED FOR THE HELP OF
YOUNG MINISTERS,

AND MAY BE SERVICEABLE TO PRIVATE CHRISTIANS,
WHO ARE ENQUIRING THE WAY TO ZION.

BY SOLOMON STODDARD, A.M.
FORMERLY PASTOR OF THE CHURCH IN
NORTHAMPTON, MASSACHUSETTS

WITH AN
EPISTLE PREFIXED
BY THE
REV. DR. INCREASE MATHER

Soli Deo Gloria Publications
...for instruction in righteousness...

Soli Deo Gloria Publications
213 W. Vincent Street, Ligonier, PA 15658-1139
(412) 238-7741/FAX (412) 238-3002

*

A Guide to Christ
was first reprinted in Northampton in 1816.
This Soli Deo Gloria reprint is copyrighted 1993.

*

ISBN 1-877611-55-7

CONTENTS

APPENDIX

EDITOR'S NOTE

Soli Deo Gloria Publications is pleased to offer this book by Solomon Stoddard, hoping that it will help the church rediscover the doctrine of "seeking" or "preparation." What once was widely accepted as Reformed evangelism has now largely been lost, except for a few who have helped keep it alive.

This was the teaching of the English and American Puritans. You will find it in the writings and sermons of William Perkins, Richard Sibbes, Richard Greenham, Thomas Goodwin, and many others. Jonathan Edwards preached this doctrine here in America, and so did his grandfather, Solomon Stoddard, as you will read.

We do not endorse everything by Stoddard because we have reprinted this book . We are in disagreement with his teaching on the "Half-Way Covenant" and "Converting Ordinances." In that vein, we stand with Jonathan Edwards. You will find some of this teaching in the final sermon in our appendix, a sermon magnificently titled, "The Inexcusableness of Neglecting the Worship of God Under a Pretense of being in an Unconverted Condition."

We have chosen to include that sermon with this work because of its great significance in understanding historically the teaching about "Converting Ordinances," and to help better understand the controversy that finally caused the dismissal of Jonathan Edwards from his church in Northampton. We encourage the reader to read this portion carefully and with discernment. There is much here that is a feast for the soul, however. Enjoy this classic!

Don Kistler
Soli Deo Gloria Publications
Ligonier, PA
December 1992

INTRODUCTION

Solomon Stoddard (1643-1729), called the "pope of western Massachusetts" in his own day, is usually known today only as the grandparent of his assistant pastor, Jonathan Edwards. Moreover, it is his unique and original ecclesiastical ideas, that deviated drastically from traditional reformed patterns, that were to cause Edwards' dismissal after twenty-three years of remarkable ministry in Northampton.

Because "Stoddardianism" was so famous historically, let me detail the steps of his theological thinking.

1. In 1679, the Reforming Synod was shocked to hear Stoddard not only defend "Half-Way Covenant" thinking, but advocate what came to be called "Converting Ordinances."

2. This doctrine stated that persons who confessed faith in Christ and were free of scandalous living (without necessarily relating their "experiences") were to be admitted to communion. Those who could not confidently relate their experiences had previously been denied communicant membership, though their children could receive baptism. Stoddard would admit their parents to the Lord's Supper.

3. Though the Synod was shocked, it went reluctantly along, Increase Mather dissenting.

4. In 1700, Stoddard's *Instituted Churches* spelled out the "Converting Ordinances" doctrine. By 1704, Stoddard was avowing it fully to his congregation; and by 1709 he explained things to Increase Mather's satisfaction.

5. Later works solidified Stoddardianism. In 1729, his *The Safety of Appearing in the Righteousness of Christ at the Day of Judgment* was his final statement before his own appearing before his Lord at death.

6. In July, 1750, Jonathan Edwards preached his farewell sermon at Northampton, dismissed because of his

break with "Stoddardianism."

7. By the end of the century, "Converting Ordinances" became virtually extinct.

This *Guide to Christ* shows Solomon Stoddard at his very best. He may have been in error on "Converting Ordinances," but this little book is a guide to the finest Reformed theology. He may have been wrong in guiding to the Lord's Table, but not in guiding to the Lord Himself.

The only trouble with this *Guide* is that it is too good! Our century is not worthy of it or its author. Even in its advanced day (nearly 300 years ago), it was written for "young ministers," and not for those they guided. Today, even our ministers are hardly equal to it. Yet they and we all must become so. It is a classic.

If "young ministers" (and old) are Christ's appointed guides to Christ, they would do well to take and master this seminary course by Professor Stoddard. If they do so, multitudes of their parishioners are going to find it "SERVICEABLE TO PRIVATE CHRISTIANS WHO ARE ENQUIRING THE WAY TO ZION."

John H. Gerstner
Ligonier, PA
November 1992

TO THE READER

That preparation for Christ is necessary before the soul can be united by Him to faith is an undoubted truth. He *came not to call the righteous, but sinners to repentance.* Men must be convinced of their being sinners or they will not be in bitterness for it. Sin must be bitter to them or they will not forsake it. As long as they love their sins, it is impossible that they should believe on Christ, John 5:44, nor will they come to Christ for righteousness and life unless they have a humbling sense of their own unrighteousness, Romans 10:3.

These are truths which cannot be denied; but whether there is any preparatory work, which is saving before faith, has been controverted among divines. My learned tutor (whom for honor's sake I mention), Mr. John Norton (once a famous teacher in Boston), in his <u>Orthodox Evangelist</u>, Chapter 8, has elaborately proved the negative, with whom the worthy author of the ensuing discourse concurs. It has been an error (and a tyrannical one) in some preachers that they have made their own particular experiences a standard for all others when as God is pleased to use a great variety in bringing His elect home to Christ, although conversion, as to the subject of it, is the same in all who are brought into a state of salvation.

Some have experienced such terrors and distress of conscience as others have not been acquainted with who, nevertheless, are true believers on Christ. To that question, "What measure of preparatory work is necessary to conversion?" Mr. Norton answers judiciously, "As the greatest measure has no necessary connection with salvation, so the least measure puts the soul into a preparatory capacity, or ministerial disposition to the receiving of Christ. There is not the same degree of humiliation in all those who are converted, for some feel a greater measure of trouble, others a lesser, but all who are truly converted are humbled."

Nor can it be determined how long a man must be held under fears and terrors before he is truly converted. To affirm that men must be so many years or months under a spirit of bondage before they can believe on Christ is contrary to the experience of many pious souls and to the Scriptures. The preparatory work of the converts mentioned in the sacred writings was not of long continuance. That super-eminent divine, Dr. Thomas Goodwin, in his preface to Mr. Hooker's work on preparation, observes that "a man may be held too long under John the Baptist's water," and that some have urged too far and insisted too much on that as preparatory which includes the beginning of true faith.

Such authors as have asserted that men cannot be sincere converts unless they have been under great legal terrors for some considerable time have caused groundless fears and perplexity in the minds of many gracious souls, for the relief of whom Reverend Mr. Giles Firmin published an excellent book entitled <u>The Real Christian</u>. Very often the children of godly parents, who have had a religious education and have been kept from all scandalous sins that wound and waste the conscience, have been favored with an easy, as well as an early, conversion. The seed of grace has sprung up in their hearts, *they know not how,* Matthew 4:27. So as that although they can say, as the blind man restored to his sight did, "now I see," yet the particular time they cannot account for.

Says Mr. Norton, "It is our duty to bless God that we are converted, and not groundlessly to afflict ourselves about the time of our conversion." And he cites Mr. William Pemble, whose words are, "To tell the month, day, or hour wherein they were converted is, in most converts, impossible; in all, of exceeding difficult observation; though I deny not but the time may be, in some, of sensible mark."

That eminent man of God, Mr. Richard Baxter, in his treatise on infant baptism, relates that he was once at a meeting of many Christians as eminent for holiness as most in the land, of whom divers were ministers of great fame, and it was desired that every one of them would give an account of the time and manner of his conversion. There was but one of them all that could do it! And, he says, "I avow from my heart that I neither know the day, nor the year, when I began to be sincere." Nevertheless, for the most part, they who have been great sinners are not converted without great terrors of conscience.

Our great Mr. Hooker (of whom Dr. Goodwin says that if any man in this age came in the spirit of John the Baptist, Hooker was that man), his doctrine will be found a sad truth, viz. "that as for gross and scandalous sinners, God usually exercises them with heavy breakings of heart before they are brought to Christ." Especially it is so if the Lord intends to make use of them in great services for His name. Saul, afterwards Paul, had a terrible conversion, although he was not long in the pangs of the new birth. The like has not been noted of Luther.

The famous Mr. John Rogers of Dedham had been very extravagant in his youth. Mr. Richard Rogers of Weathersfield, who was his kinsman, helped to maintain him at the University where he sold his books and spent the money so that his kinsman and patron would have utterly cast him off had not the entreaties of a near relation prevailed with him to try him once again. When he saw what a wonderful change converting grace had made on his young kinsman, he would often say, "I will never despair of a man for John Roger's sake." God designed that this very ungodly youth should be made a great instrument of glory to His name, and of good to many of His elect. He was bruised to no purpose under the hand of the Almighty. Great were the terrors of his soul for some time when he would get alone under bushes in the field, praying and crying to God for mercy. When he was converted, it is thought he was an instrument of converting more souls than any one minister in England. He was inspired with an extraordinary zeal; he had a way of delivering himself in his sermons which, in any other man, would have been ridiculous, but in him it was very becoming and awful, which made Bishop Browning say to Mr. Ward, "John Rogers will do more with his wild note than we shall do with all our set music."

But this is God's usual method with such of His elect as have fallen into great sins. He brings them home by great terrors. For the confirmation of this, I might have instanced Mr. Robert Bolton, whose excellent books have made him famous in the church of God. Before his conversion, he was very wicked. He loved stage plays, cards, and dice. He was a horrible swearer, Sabbath-breaker, a boon companion who neither loved God nor good men. He hated Puritanical preaching. Hearing the same of Mr. William Perkins, he went to Cambridge to hear him preach and, having heard him, said, "He was a barren, empty fellow, and a passing mean scholar." This man, after his conversion, was an eminent saint and a successful minister of Jesus Christ. but the manner of his conversion was terrible. His sins were so heavy upon him that he roared for anguish of heart. He would sometimes rise out of bed in the night for anguish of spirit and, to augment his misery, he was afflicted with grievous temptations. These heart-piercing sorrows continued for many months. They issued in a sound conversion.

There have been some who have maintained that a man is not sufficiently prepared for Christ unless he is brought to that place where he is, out of respect to the will and glory of God, content to be damned eternally. A horrid assertion, justly disclaimed by the author of this present discourse, and refuted by The Orthodox Evangelist, yet there are some unhappy passages of that nature in a book of "humiliation," which goes under Mr. Hooker's name, by which incredible wrong has been done to that great author. It may be that it will be to the satisfaction of some readers to see what Dr. Goodwin has written concerning Mr. Hookers' books about "preparation for Christ," who, in his epistle prefixed to Mr. Hooker's sermons on Acts 2:37 has these words:

> There has been published long since many parts and pieces of this author upon this argument, sermon-wise, preached by him here in England, yet having been taken by an unskillful hand, upon his recess into these remoter parts of the world, was bold, without his privity or consent, to print and published them (one of the greatest injuries that can be done to any man). It came to pass that his genuine meaning, and this in points of so high a nature, and in some things different from the common opinion, was diverted in those printed sermons from the fair and clear draft of his own notions and intentions, because so utterly deformed and misrepresented in multitudes of passages and in the rest, but imperfectly and crudely set forth.

That which the Doctor says is a sufficient vindication of the renowned name of Mr. Hooker from the reflections cast upon him on the account of some rude expressions in those books pretended to be his, which were never printed with his allowance.

The like is to be said with references to some passage in Mr. Thomas Shepard's Sincere Convert, which has occasioned some great disquietment in some godly minds, and made them afraid to believe on Christ when deeply sensible of their misery without Him. Concerning this book, Mr. Shepard wrote a letter to Mr. Firmin dated December 27, 1647, and expressed himself thus, "That which is called The Sincere Convert, I have not the book. I once saw it; it was a collection of such notes in a dark town in England which one procuring of me published them without my will or privity; nor do I like to see it. He that published it confesseth it came out altered from what was first written."

It is usual with new converts to be molested with fears lest they have committed the sin of the Holy Ghost. I am far from being of Dr. John Tillotson's opinion who supposed that none in these days are, or can be, guilty of that sin, nor any besides those, who were eye-witnesses of the miracles wrought by our Savior Christ. I rather concur with Dr. John Collings, whose words are, "Give me leave to speak my fears. These are my thoughts, that we live in an age as full of persons who have sinned that sin which shall never be forgiven as any age ever was since our Lord was on earth."

Are there not many in our days who, having been once enlightened, have not only sinned against the light of their education, but have become malignant haters of those holy truths and ways of God in which they were initiated, and malicious persecutors of all such as profess the true and pure gospel? Do not such sin willfully after they have received the knowledge of the truth? And have they not done despite to the Spirit of Grace? As for such as are troubled with groundless fears of their having been guilty of that sin, the reverend author of the discourse emitted herewith has therein offered that which may ease and satisfy their disquieted consciences. Mr. Baxter notwithstanding the dispute which had been him and Mr. Tombs about paedobaptism, after that wrote a commendatory epistle before a learned book of Mr. Tombs against the Papists.

It is known that in some circles (not fundamentals in religion) I differ from this beloved author. Nevertheless, as when there was a difference of opinion between Jerome and Austin, Jerome said for all that, "I cannot but love Christ in Austin." So do I say concerning my brother Stoddard. And I pray the Lord to bless this, and all his holy labors for the conversion and salvation of many of God's elect.

INCREASE MATHER
November 15, 1714

PREFACE

The work of regeneration being of absolute necessity unto salvation, it greatly concerns ministers especially, in all ways possible, to promote the same; and in particular that they guide souls aright who are under a work of preparation. There are some who deny any necessity of the preparatory work of the Spirit of God in order to a closing with Christ. This is a very dark cloud, both as it is an evidence that men do not have the experience of that work in their own souls, and as it is a sign that such men are utterly unskillful in guiding others who are under this work. If this opinion should prevail in the land, it would give a deadly wound to religion. It would expose men to think of themselves as converted when they are not.

If men understand that there is a work of humiliation before faith, then, if they get some common affections (love, sorrow, delight, yes, and a common faith too), they will say that these are not of the right kind; for men must see the plague of their own hearts, their helplessness, and that they are like the clay in the hand of the potter before they come to Christ, and so will be afraid and be searching themselves. But if they do not know any necessity of preparation, they will take the first appearance of holiness for holiness; and, if they find religious affections in themselves, they will grow confident that God has wrought a good work in them. It would, likewise, expose them to bolster up others in false confidence.

A man who knows there must be a work of preparation will be careful how he encourages others that they are in Christ. He will inquire how God has made way for their receiving of Christ; but another who is a stranger to it will be ready to take all for gold that glitters and, if he sees men religiously disposed, will be speaking peace to them. He will be like the false prophets saying, *peace, peace, when there is no peace.* So men will be hardened. It is a dismal thing to give men sleepy notions and make them sleep the sleep of death.

The truth of this opinion is much to be suspected from what has been left on record to the contrary by Arthur Hildersham, William Perkins, John Dodd, Richard Sibbes, Daniel Dyke, John Ball, John Preston, Thomas Hooker, Thomas Shepard, John Norton, and others of the like stamp, whose judgment in matters of this nature outweighs the judgment of thousands of others, though otherwise learned men. But, besides this, there is a great deal of light in the Word of God in this matter. I will not argue from Israel's being led by Moses the lawgiver out of Egypt, through a land of pits and droughts and fiery flying serpents, before they were brought into the land of Canaan by Joshua; nor from the legal dispensation of the covenant of grace foregoing the evangelical; nor from John the Baptist's being sent as a forerunner of Christ to prepare the way of the Lord; nor from the parable of the Prodigal being in want and becoming a servant of a citizen of the country before he returned to his father; nor from the dry bones being in a disconsolate condition before God put life into them. These things may be better made use of for illustrations than proofs.

But then there are other Scriptures which hold forth that there must be preparation for Christ before our closing with Him. It appears by instances recorded in the Scripture. One is of Paul, Acts 9:4-5. He was terrified, in way of preparation, to his receiving Christ, and about the same time was led to the understanding of his own helplessness, Romans 7:9. Another is of the jailer, Acts 16:29-31. He was greatly scared lest he should fall short of salvation; and, since we have such instances, and none to the contrary, we may judge that this is God's method in converting sinners.

It also appears from such doctrines as are held forth in Scripture that some sinners are near the kingdom of God, and some are far from it. Mark 12:34 shows that some men are in a more prepared way, and more hopeful to receive it, than others. So that doctrine that some are not in a present capacity to come to Christ because they are under the power of a carnal design, John 5:44, shows that men must be broken off from their carnal designs before they come to Christ. So the doctrine of the difficulty of getting into a state of salvation, Matthew 8:13 and Luke 13:24, shows that there are many difficulties in the way of conversion and that, by striving, they may get into a nearer preparedness for faith.

It also appears by that prophecy of our Savior, where it is foretold that God will first prepare men and then bring them to Christ, John 16:8. Here it is foretold what method the Spirit will take with men. He will not reveal the righteousness of Christ to men in the first place. In order to do this, He convinces them of sin and makes them see their danger and miserable condition. First he searches the wound and then applies the remedy.

It also appears by the particular application of the call of the gospel to those who are prepared. Sometimes the call is propounded generally to all, but at other times it is propounded particularly to such as are in distress by reason of their sins, who see themselves as miserable and undone, Matthew 11:38, Isaiah 55:1, Revelation 22:17. The call is applied particularly to these as being in the next capacity to give entertainment unto it, intimating the good condition that men must be in before they receive it.

Experience also gives considerable light in this matter. We learn by experience that men's hearts are generally set for carnal things before they are terrified, and for their own righteousness before they see their own hearts. Generally, such men who have not had the terrors of God in them don't much mind eternal things. If they are not rude and vicious, they are worldly, vain, and proud, Ephesians 2:3. And such convinced sinners as have not been led into the understanding of their hearts are set to build up a righteousness of their own. They are taking encouragement from their frames, with a neglect of Christ. Experience also shows that many men, highly reputed of for religion, have had a work of preparation. Many men who have a special interest in the hearts of others can give a fair account how they have been prepared for Christ, and many professors who have not had such experience have not proved well. Several who had some light touches of conviction, though they have made a blaze for awhile, yet have proved themselves carnal men at last, or at least have rendered themselves suspect. Many who have been strangers to the work of preparation have cracked their credit at last, Matthew 13:20-21.

Yes, many godly people know that they were hypocrites and never saw Christ until after they had a work of humiliation. They know they were not godly, though they have affections, enlargements, and encouragements. It was all common work, and they had not spark of grace in them. Their religion was but the fruit of nature improved, Romans 7:9.

Yes, this is exceedingly agreeable to reason. The light of nature cannot give a demonstration of it for it is a voluntary dispensation. There is no necessity in nature of any preparation before the infusion of grace. Christ changed the water into wine and raised the dead to life without any previous preparation, so He can do it in this case. The work of preparation does not make the work of the new creation the easier, for after men have a work of preparation, sin reigns in them as much as before. Preparation does not at all destroy the principle, and men, when prepared, can do nothing to help God in planting grace in them; and men who are not prepared can do nothing to hinder God in implanting grace. But it is very agreeable to reason that the Spirit does a work of preparation before it infuses grace; for it is the duty of ministers to preach such things to sinners as are proper to work this preparation. They are bound to preach the threatenings of the law, man's insufficiency, and God's sovereignty. Yes, the manner of God is to deal with men after the manner of men. Man is a rational creature and, therefore, God deals with him in a moral way, setting convictions before him. Men would make enemies submit before they pardon them, so does God. Besides, it is the duty of the sinner to do those things wherein preparation consists. It is their duty to reform and to make an absolute resignation of themselves to God. No wonder, then, if God holds them to it. Yes, further, there is an absolute necessity in nature that men be prepared before the exercise of faith. Men cannot exercise faith until the heart is prepared by a sense of danger and the insufficiency of other things. If they don't see their danger, they can see no occasion that they have come to Christ. If they don't see themselves liable to wrath, how can they come to Christ to save them from wrath? As long as they imagine that they can help themselves, they will not come to Christ for help. Men can't trust in Christ alone until they are driven out of themselves. They cannot come as helpless and undone until they see themselves so, Philippians 3:3.

And seeing there is such a work of preparation foregoing men's closing with Christ, it must be of great consequence for awakened sinners to be guided aright under this work. If men have the best guides, yet they may miscarry, but undoubtedly many do perish for lack of suitable help. Some, after they have been in trouble awhile, grow discouraged under apprehensions that their seeking will be in vain, and so leave off endeavoring after a converted state. Some wander up and down under fears and hopes as the children of Israel in the wilderness until they die. They cannot be quiet in a way of sin, neither can they find the way of deliverance. And many others, after a little trouble, are comforted under a notion of being at peace with God. Unskillful surgeons make a palliate cure and persuade them that the bitterness of death is past. Multitudes of souls perish through the ignorance of those who should guide them in the way to heaven. Men are nourished up with vain hopes of being in a state of salvation before they have got half the way to Christ.

Those, therefore, whose business it is to lead souls to Christ need to furnish themselves with skill and understanding to handle wounded consciences in a right manner so that they may be serviceable to them in their distresses. Who would venture his ship with an unskillful pilot? Who would venture his wounded body with an unskillful surgeon? Who would willingly put his distressed soul into the hands of an unskillful minister? Men should not satisfy themselves with other points of learning, but labor so that they may speak words in season to everyone that is weary, that, as Moses said to his father-in-law, they *may be instead of eyes to them that are in the wilderness.*

There are two things especially serviceable to this end.

One is that they get experience of this word in their own hearts. If they have no experience, they will be but blind guides. They will be in great danger to entertain false notions concerning a work of conversion. They will be inclined to think that there is not so much necessary as in order to conversion. They are in danger of being deceived with pretenses of men's being delivered from their own righteousness with shows of humiliation, faith, and love. Whatever books men have read, there is great need of experimental knowledge in a minister. Many particular things will occur that he will not meet with in books. It is a great calamity to wounded consciences to be under the direction of an inexperienced minister.

The other is to be acquainted with the observations of those who have traveled much in this work. If a man has experience in his own soul, that experience will not reach all cases that may come before him. There is a great variety in the workings of the Spirit, and men that have had to do with many souls in their distresses may afterward meet with such difficulties as may puzzle them very much. Therefore, it is of great use to get the knowledge of the observations of those men who have had to do with great variety of cases, whereby they may get a larger understanding how to manage themselves when things are difficultly circumstanced.

This small treatise, composed upon the desire of younger ministers, is offered to the consideration of such as desire to be further instructed in the right way of dealing with distressed souls, and if the author shall be hereby the instrument of the salvation of any perishing souls, he shall count his labor well bestowed.

Solomon Stoddard

Directions How to Guide Souls Through the Work of Conversion

When a sinner, wounded in spirit, applies himself unto a minister of the gospel for counsel, it is profitable, after some inquiries concerning the time, means, and degree of their convictions and terrors, to use this method with him:

1. To confirm and establish him in the apprehensions of the dangerousness of a natural condition, showing him that every man who dies in a state of nature will certainly be damned, that a state of damnation is intolerable, that the continuance of his opportunities for deliverance is very uncertain; for there is danger that if his convictions are not cherished, they may by degrees wear off. Many men's terrors are but short-lived. They harden their hearts by company, clogging themselves with worldly business and their natural disposition to flatter themselves.

2. Encourage him to be in the use of means in order to his conversion; for, if they do not have hopes of obtaining mercy, either they will not seek after it or they will do it in such a careless and dull way that it will come to nothing. God leads men through the whole work of preparation partly by fear and partly by hope. If they run into either extreme, to have fear without hope or hope without fear, they are like a ship that goes beside the channel and is in danger of being broken to pieces. A mixture of fear and hope makes men diligent. They may be encouraged from such considerations as these: that God has provided a glorious way of salvation through Christ so that all who believe in Him shall be saved; that there is an infinite ocean of mercy in the heart of God; that God has had compassion on many greater sinners than they; that the day of grace is not yet gone; that God is now striving with them by His Spirit, which is many times the forerunner of conversion.

3. To direct him what course to take at present; as:

(1) Daily to seek God in secret. As this is a duty, so it is a special means to cherish the motions of God's Spirit in his heart. If this is neglected, it would be no wonder if his convictions should die away. He is also to be directed, not to content himself in putting up some good requests to God, but he should open his case plainly before God as he would to a physician if he were sick. This is a way to keep him from wandering thoughts in prayer, and further to affect his own soul with his condition. Isaiah 55:6, *Seek ye the Lord while He may be found.*

(2) To reform his life, and not to indulge himself in any sins of omission or commission in any external sins, nor in doing good actions in a sinful manner. Men who are seeking salvation must not allow themselves to go on in a way of damnation. That terror is not sufficient that will suffer men to live an unreformed life. If men are thoroughly scared, they will dread doing what wounds their consciences. Fear of hell will make men afraid to sin. If they are thoroughly wounded, those temptations that formerly carried them away will be overcome, Luke 13:10-14.

(3) To lay himself open to the convictions of the Spirit. Sometimes men are desirous to be convinced and terrified, but not too much. They will overrule their convictions as to time and degree; but, as a patient leaves himself in the hands of the surgeon, so should they leave themselves in the hand of the Spirit, when it pleases Him and as much as it pleases Him, not shutting their eyes against the light, John 3:20.

After the awakened sinner has been using means awhile, he oftentimes gives an account of some alteration. He finds some affections, sorrow for sin, delight in Sabbaths, love to the people of God, love to reading of the Scripture. What is to be said to him in this case?

1. He is to be told that he must not rest in ease, but

labor after healing. If a wise man, by applying plasters to a sore, is delivered from much of the anguish he was in, he will not satisfy himself with that and give over the use of means, lest the anguish should return again. So the sinner needs to be careful that he does not satisfy himself in the ease of his conscience, but must get it healed by the application of the blood of Jesus Christ.

2. It is extremely dangerous to tell him that it is hopeful that God has put the seeds of grace into him. There is not one in a thousand but experiences such religious affections long before he is converted. These religious affections are nothing else but the workings of self-love and natural conscience. Natural conscience discovers the danger of sin and something of the baseness of it; hence he is sorry for it. The man conceives some hope that by praying, reading, etc., he shall get salvation. Hence he delights in them. The man hopes that he has been accepted by God, hence he has some affections to Him. And, if a minister speaks encouragingly, as if the man were converted, he lays a foundation for his ruin, for he is in great danger to fall in with the flattery.

3. He is to be warned against a self-righteous spirit. Men are exceedingly ready to think that their good works and religious frames will abate the fierce anger of God and incline God to pity them and have mercy on them. They are proud of their services, ignorant of the righteousness of Christ and of the freedom of God's mercy. They think God cannot love them unless they are lovely, and that He cannot *but* love them if they are lovely, and so they are ready to dote upon their own righteousness. Romans 10:3, *They go about to establish their own righteousness.* Therefore, the man is to be warned against this, and light is to be held forth to him to convince him of the insufficiency thereof.

4. He may be put upon to examine these affections, whether or not they are hypocritical. And signs may be given to him whereby he may discern them to be so; but there needs to be great care that the signs are sound and

warranted by the Word of God. Otherwise, he is in danger of being established in his mistake.

QUESTION 1. Are sinners who are awakened to be directed to labor to work up their hearts to sincere sorrow for sin and love to God and Jesus Christ?

ANSWER 1. If their terrors are great, they are ready of themselves to labor to do this from a self-righteous spirit. That they may win the heart of God and assuage His anger, they commonly take a great deal of pains in order thereto, that they may work up gracious qualifications in themselves. They set spiritual considerations before themselves, read and hear, and use all the methods that are in their power to cultivate their own hearts.

ANSWER 2. It is a presumptuous thing for them to strive for this, for it is impossible for them to work up such things in their own hearts. They are dead in sins and cannot sanctify themselves. No principle that they have will produce such an effect. Fear will not make them do it. The fear of hell cannot make men hate sin more than hell. Self-love will not make them love God above themselves. They cannot, by consideration, work any such effect upon their hearts, for they do not understand spiritual things. Encouragements will not make them do it, for it is beyond their power. Resolutions will be ineffectual. They may as easily remove mountains as do this. Therefore, it is that they should not strive to work their own hearts to it.

ANSWER 3. There can be no benefit of such direction except this, that they may bind by experience their own inability; that, after they have done their utmost, they may by their own experience understand their own helplessness. It is the duty of men to love God and to repent of sin; and it is the duty of sinners to labor that they may love God and repent of sin, etc., but it is not in their power to work up their hearts to the love of God and godly sorrow. They should labor to be convinced that they cannot do it.

SOMETIMES, it is much to be suspected, that they do not reform all that is amiss, and in this case:

1. The danger of a natural condition is to be solemnly set before them. Though their terrors seem to be great, yet they need to be greater. Men must have so much terror as to bring them to a separation from sin. Therefore, there is need to represent their danger in the most lively and dreadful way so that the sense thereof may pierce their heart deeply. If they are but thoroughly scared, they will be brought to a universal reformation, Isaiah 2:20-21.

2. They are to be urged to reformation. Their duty in this matter is to be particularly pressed upon them. Their consciences must be stirred to part with all sin as Christ urged the Jews, Matthew 5:29, *If thy right eye offend thee, pluck it out.* For the neglect of reformation will put a stop to the work, and they will not get forward in the work of humiliation until they are reformed. As the first concoction prepares for the second, so reformation does for humiliation. Men must overcome the next and more immediate difficulties before they overcome those that are remote. He who will not part with sinful practices will not yield himself into the hands of justice. If they do not reform, they put the work to a stand. Yes, such men aggravate their own sorrows, for trouble will lie upon them until their hearts are brought to be humbled, and their terrors will be multiplied, if they belong to God, until they are persuaded to reform. Psalm 32:3, *When I kept silence, my bones waxed old through my roaring all the day.*

SOMETIMES, some particular sin lies exceedingly heavy on his heart. In this case the minister may tell him:

1. That it is not his duty in ordinary cases to publish such sin to him; it is fit that he should confess it to God. But ordinarily there is no just occasion to publish a scandal to him. It is best that secret sins be kept secret unless the circumstances of the person call for making it known.

2. That the sin is pardonable. This he may demonstrate from several examples in the Scripture: from the sufficiency of Christ's redemption, from several offers and promises of the gospel, that the man's heart may not sink with discouragement.

3. That in case the rule does call for any satisfaction to men, he must not delay that but that must be attended as soon as there is opportunity. If he can make satisfaction without confession, there is no necessity for confession; for satisfaction answers for the wrong that has been done to a man.

4. That he must not be sensible of that sin only, but of all other sins. Every sin is provoking to God and deserving of damnation, and particularly that his impenitency and unbelief is more dangerous than any former act of sin. John 3:19, *This is the condemnation, that light is come into the world, and men love darkness rather than light.*

SOMETIMES, after the man has been in trouble awhile and before he has any great experience of his own heart, he has some promises come to him with a great deal of refreshing, and he hopes God has accepted him. In this case, the minister may tell him:

1. That it is a common thing for God to give encouragements unto men before they are carried through the work of conversion. As God gives them encouragements by His Word, so He does, many times, by His Spirit. God always maintains, in the hearts of sinners who are seeking Him, some hopes that they may obtain mercy; and sometimes He gives them a very great refreshing by some sense of the glory of heaven, Luke 14:15, by some superficial discoveries of Christ, Matthew 13:20, thereby holding forth some promises before them. The design of these is to draw them on a way of seeking, and to support them under their temptations.

2. That God never gives a faith of assurance before He

gives a faith of dependence; for He never manifests His love until men are in a state of favor and reconciliation, which is by a faith of dependence. When men have comfortable Scriptures come to them, they are apt to take them as tokens of God's love; but men must first be brought into Christ by accepting the offer of the gospel before they are fit for such manifestations. God's method is first to make the soul accept the offers of grace, and then to manifest His good estate unto him.

3. That if his comfort is not of the right kind, it will not continue and, usually after such encouragements, men's terrors are wont to return with as much violence as ever. God commonly intermingles smiles and frowns, and if such vain confidences as men took up from refreshing Scriptures are but nipped in the bud, they generally wither away, and their fears return as strong as ever.

When the sinner who was hoping he was in a good estate, because some refreshing Scriptures came to him, sees his mistake, he is in danger of being discouraged. In this case he may be told:

1. That it is a common thing for persons who are afterwards converted to pass through such changes. It is not a peculiar thing to him, but a thing of ordinary experience in such people as God is about to deliver out of a natural state. They commonly have some lightsome times, and then returns of darkness. There was no reason to expect that these should last very long. Such comforts are like Jonah's gourd; they rise in a night and perish in a night.

2. That it is a great mercy that those confidences are taken away from him. Had they continued, they would have ruined him. False confidence is better lost than kept. His condition is the more hopeful now that those confidences are lost. While he had those confidences, he was like a ship that stuck in the sand and, now that he is delivered from them, there is more ground of encouragement.

After he has had affliction and enlargement for awhile, he is wont to complain that he grows more dull and he is afraid that his convictions are about to leave him. In this case he may be told:

1. That there is no reason to expect that his convictions should always be in the like degree. Persons in such a condition are subject to many alterations as it is with a ship at sea. Sometimes it has a fair wind, sometimes it blows more moderately, sometimes it is calm. Yes, sometimes it has storms and cross winds. There are many changes that pass over such men. So men in a journey sometimes have a good way, sometimes bad. They meet with rivers and miry places where they cannot make speed.

2. That he must be very careful that he does nothing to quench the motions of the Spirit, I Thessalonians 5:19. There are many ways whereby men do it: sometimes by discouragement, sometimes by presumption and flattery, sometimes by rebelling against the light, sometimes by company keeping. Men who are addicted to company commonly lose these convictions as do men by crowding themselves with worldly business. Though diligence is no hindrance, yet cumbering themselves will be a great impediment to the abiding of convictions.

3. That it is his best way to improve the convictions that he has. Sometimes, persons are wont to argue that it will be to no purpose for them to strive. If they do not have greater convictions, they shall but tire themselves to no purpose, and they conceive it best for them to tarry until they have stronger convictions; but the seaman is wont to hoist his sails and improve the wind he has, whether it be less or more. If men improve moderate convictions, they may get forward and do that which will further their conversion and, if they improve lesser convictions, that is the way to have more. It is their duty to do it, and in that way God owns them. *To him that hath shall be given.* Some who have complained of the smallness of their convictions have,

within a while, changed their note and complained as much of the greatness of them, that they have been such that they could hardly live under them.

A person who is under the work of conversion is subject to many assignments and discouraging temptations; a dreadful sound is in his ears. All such persons do not have the same temptations, and they do not have them in any certain order; but care must be taken to give suitable support, and advice to them according to the variety of their temptations.

One temptation is that he is not elected; that God has overlooked him and appointed him to condemnation. This sometimes lies upon the heart with great weight. In this case he may be told:

1. That those things that make him fear that he is not elected are no certain signs of it. There are no certain tokens of reprobation upon him. Those things that he takes to be signs are very uncertain. The greatness of his sins do not argue reprobation. Many who have been guilty of great sins have been elected. His being of elderly years does not argue it. Sometimes God turns such to Himself, Malachi 4:5-6. God's leaving him still in a natural estate, though he has sought God a long time, does not show it. Israel was a great while traveling from Egypt to Canaan.

2. That it is a sinful thing for him to draw any conclusions about his election. It is a secret reserved in God's own breast, and he cannot determine anything understandingly about it. Deuteronomy 29:29, *Secret things belong unto the Lord our God.* When he undertakes to conclude that he is not elected, he acts presumptuously. His conclusion may be false for all he knows; he pretends to know what he is ignorant of.

3. That God's striving with him by His Spirit is a hopeful sign that he is elected, for many times it is the fruit of election. When the Spirit convinces of sin, it is in order to His convincing of righteousness, John 16:8. This is the

course that God is wont to take with those who are elected. Frequently, He lets reprobates live in security, but He is wont to terrify the elect in order to their conversion; and, the more earnestly the man follows after God and labors to get into a converted condition, the more hopeful it is that God has elected him, for where God has appointed the end, He has appointed the means also.

Another temptation is that he has committed the unpardonable sin; that he has committed the sin against the Holy Ghost, that sin which is unto death. He has carried badly after illuminations and it sinks into him that now there is no remedy.

In this case he may be told that it has been a frequent thing for men to fear that they have committed this sin who have, afterwards, been converted; that it is not the manner of those who have committed that sin to be perplexed and exercised with fears about it, but the principal way to help in this case is to inform him from the Word of God what this sin is. Particularly, he may be informed:

1. That it is an external sin, not a sin that is committed in the heart. Men have some wicked thoughts after enlightenings and then fear that they have been guilty of that sin, but that is an outward sin. It is a sin that other men may see, I John 5:16.

2. That it is a course of sin, not any particular act of sin which a man breaks off from and is troubled for, but a way of evil that he continues impenitently in.

3. That it is one particular sort of sin, committed with great aggravations; namely, a rejecting of the profession of the gospel. There are many other grievous sins, but none of them, however aggravated, are the unpardonable sin. It is a rejecting of the truth of the gospel and renouncing the profession. Therefore, they are said to *fall away,* Hebrews 6:6. They are said to *forsake the assemblies of the people of God,* Hebrews 10:25. They are said to *tread under foot the son of God,* and *to deny their baptism,* Hebrews 10:29. So

that if any person among us should turn papist or heathen, having a blasphemous spirit against the ways of God and a bloody, persecuting spirit towards the people of God, there might be reason to fear that he was guilty of the unpardonable sin. But there are no footsteps in the Scripture to judge that men who are following after God and laboring to get into a converted condition have committed that sin, though they are guilty of much unbelief, of many decays and backslidings, and of very vile thoughts and risings of heart; for multitudes of men who have been guilty of such things have had experience afterwards of the pardoning grace of God.

Another temptation is that his day of grace is past. He had a time when he might have obtained mercy, but he has let it slip, and it is in vain for him to strive. In this case the minister may tell him:

1. That it is a common device of Satan, when he cannot persuade men that it is too soon, then to persuade them that it is too late. He is set to hinder men from using means; and first he tells them there is no haste and, when that temptation will do no longer, he changes his voice and tells them that the season is gone.

2. That there is no such doctrine in the Scripture that any sort of men's day of grace is past before the day of life is past unless they are guilty of the unpardonable sin. It is taught in Scripture that God will strive with some men only a limited time and then destroy them, Genesis 6:3, *My Spirit shall not always strive with man, yet his days shall be a hundred and twenty years.* It is also taught that God hardens some nations in order to great misery, Isaiah 6:10-11, and sometimes in order to their "unchurching," John 12:40. It is also taught that God may harden some particular persons before death, and never more strive with them in any remarkable way, Revelation 22:11, *Let him that is filthy be filthy still.* But there is no such thing taught that there is any sort of men who may be described, or any particular person

who may be known unto himself or others, whose day of grace can be said to be past before his death. When men say their day is past, they only fear it. They do not know it.

3. That such Scriptures as seem to evidence that their day is past do not determine any such thing. It is said in Proverbs 29:1, *that he that being often reproved hardeneth his neck, shall suddenly be destroyed.* But it is evident that God waits longer upon some persons than upon others. Some threatenings are universal and some are indefinite, showing what God does many times. So it is said, Hebrews 10:28, *If any man draw back, My soul shall have no pleasure in him;* but the backsliding here spoken of seems to be the unpardonable sin. He had been speaking of that, verse 26, and seems here to have reference to the same sin; for, in other cases, God speaks encouragingly in His word unto backsliders, Jeremiah 3:22 and Hosea 14:4.

Besides the temptations mentioned, there is another sort of temptations that are very exercising to him. His conscience being guilty, he is much subject to frights.

1. One temptation is that he shall be left to some great and dreadful sins. In this case, he may be told by the minister:

(1) That one special reason of these fears is that he sees more of the badness of his heart than formerly. Men under troubles of conscience are wont to see much of the corruption of their heart, and they see that which is sufficient to lead them to all sorts of wickedness; and because God is angry with them, they are afraid he will not keep them, but avenge Himself on them by leaving them to such wickedness.

(2) That God is now striving with him in order to his eternal good. God is exercising a great deal of mercy, and he has no cause to conclude that God will so leave him. Though God might justly do it, yet he has reason to hope in God to preserve him.

(3) That it is fit he should be humbled under the

sense of the depravedness of his nature and be sensible of the insufficiency of his own righteousness, to bring him into the favor of God, his heart being a sink of all manner of sin. He can never be justified except by the perfect righteousness of Jesus Christ.

(4) That his best way is to make haste to get into a converted condition. If he were once converted, he would not be in so much danger to fall into great transgressions because he would have, then, a holy principle to resist temptations to sin, and then he would have an interest in the favor of God; and it would be more hopeful that God would preserve them.

2. Another temptation is that he shall get a false hope, and so satisfy himself that he is in a good estate when he is far from it. He understands that it is so with many, Proverbs 30:12, Revelation 3:17. In this case the minister may tell him:

(1) That he is indeed in danger of it, both because of the pride of his spirit, ready to magnify his own performances, and because of his fears of hell. The tediousness of those fears make him ready to catch at any appearances of conversion and, therefore, he needs to be exceedingly careful. It is good for him to understand what conversion is, and what preparation there must be in order thereunto. And if there are appearances to him at any time as if he were converted, his way is to examine them thoroughly and get the help of some who are skillful before he settles himself much in that persuasion.

(2) That he must leave himself, as to that matter, in the hands of God. It is beyond his own power to deliver himself. If God delights in him, He will carry him through all the difficulties of the work and show him the right way. It may be that God may have purposes of grace to him and, if so, He will show him the path of life.

3. Another is that Satan will appear to him. This is a great terror to him, especially when he is possessed with

this fear when he withdraws himself to secret prayers. Sometimes this makes him neglect his duty; sometimes it makes him attend it with distraction. In this case the minister may tell him:

(1) That he is under God's keeping and that, when he is doing his duty, he is under God's protection. There is less reason to be afraid of Satan's appearing at that time than at many other times. It is not God's manner to suffer Satan to appear at such times.

(2) That if Satan had power and liberty to appear to him, it is not probable that he would frighten him with the expectations of it. He would not give such notice of his coming; but his design in terrifying him is to prevent him from doing that which might be serviceable to his soul.

(3) That it is too much honor to Satan to be so far outbid with the temptation as to change the time of his prayer; but if he cannot attend his duty suitably, and the temptation proves overbearing to him, it is better to attend the duty by daylight.

I may add to his case another that now and then happens. Suppose he says that he has heard some voice, seen some shape, or felt something on him. This I apprehend, at least sometimes, to be only the effect of a strong imagination. A strong fancy may make men to imagine such things, as it is with persons in their dreams, and with distracted persons. All sensation is in the brain and, therefore, by some disorder of that, men may think they see, feel, or hear things which they do not see, feel, or hear.

4. Another temptation is that it is best to destroy himself. Many have been urged to this. Some have attempted it and some have performed it as Judas did. In this case the minister may tell him:

(1) That the devil is very active in his temptations. Though he has that in his own heart that may lead him to it, yet it is Satan who stirs him up thereunto. The devil entered into Judas when he betrayed Christ and was not gone out of

him when he destroyed himself. The devil has a double design in it. One is to secure the man. He is afraid he shall lose him since now he is troubled about his condition and is taking pains for his salvation. Satan is jealous lest he escapes out of his hands and labors to make him destroy himself that he may presently secure him. Then there will be no danger of his running away. The other design is to bring reproach upon trouble of conscience and discourage others from giving way to convictions. If there is but one such instance in a town, it will make many others to stifle convictions lest they should come to the like end.

(2) That there is good reason to hope that he may obtain salvation. It is discouragement that leads men to such practices and, if he has but considerable hope of obtaining peace with God, there is not much danger of his hearkening to the temptation. Therefore, such things may be suggested as are proper to bear up his heart; things such as that the spirit of God is striving with him in order to his salvation; that Satan is afraid he will be saved; that his sins are no other than what God has pardoned oftentimes and the like.

(3) That it is a dreadful sin to destroy himself. It is a sin against nature; it is unthankfulness for God's mercy in saving his life. This is far worse than other sins that are very terrifying to him. This is the way to throw himself immediately into endless misery. Whatever may be said of the possibility of the salvation of such persons, there is no reason to think that one in a thousand is saved. This sin is heinous and quickly cuts off their opportunities. Such a man as is tempted to this sin would be afraid to tell a lie or profane the Sabbath. How much more reason does he have to fear this sin which will bring him immediately to eternal damnation? It is a poor remedy to deliver himself from anguish, to throw himself into that which is unspeakably greater. Certain damnation is far more dreadful than the fears by which they are oppressed. This will make their

condition much worse and not better.

SOMETIMES he complains of a self-righteous spirit; that he is ready to trust to everything he does; that especially, when he feels any affections, he is proud of them, and ready to make righteousness of them. In this case it may be profitable:

1. To convince him of the insufficiency of his own righteousness to save him; that his own righteousness will not bring him into favor with God for his own righteousness is utterly imperfect and so falls short of what the law requires. The law stands for perfect obedience, but he never did perform one perfect act of obedience. All his obedience is stained with corruption. Besides, while he is in a natural condition, he does nothing sincerely, but is a hypocrite in all his performances. And accordingly, God is so far from justifying him for the sake of them that He will not accept him, but holds him guilty for the sake of them. Besides, his own righteousness does not have the nature of satisfaction in it. There can be no satisfaction for sin but by bearing the curse of the law. Obedience is a natural debt, and cannot satisfy his contracted debts. If our obedience would have procured our acceptance, there would have been no need for the death of Christ. Christ's death would have been in vain, Galatians 2:22.

2. To direct him how to get delivered from this self-righteous spirit, viz., by getting an understanding of the badness of his own heart; for let him hear never so often of the vanity of his own righteousness, yet he will trust it until he sees he has none and can get none. A thorough discovery of his own heart will break him off from trusting in himself; for then he will see nothing in himself to trust in. He will be afraid of his own duties. His strongholds will all be thrown down; but a notional conviction of the insufficiency of his own righteousness to save him, without an experimental conviction of the badness of his heart will not

deliver him from the confidence in himself.

SOMETIMES he complains that he does everything from a spirit of self-love. He does not aim at the glory of God in anything; but fear of hell and desire of salvation are the great things that do set him on work. Were it not for fear of hell, he should leave off. In this case he may be told,

1. That it is impossible he should act from a higher principle. He has no principle of love to God, John 5:42. Self-love is the reigning principle in him and, therefore, it is no wonder that he does all in religion from that spirit. It was his weakness that he formerly thought he did anything out of love to God. No natural man ever acted with a higher spirit than self-love. A bad tree cannot bring forth good fruit.

2. That he should make use of this for humiliation and not for discouragement. There is no reason that he should be discouraged because of this, for every one is a hypocrite at first. And many who have sought God for awhile with a selfish spirit have afterward been turned and have had another spirit given to them; but he should make use of this to his humiliation and learn hereby his own badness, the insufficiency of his own righteousness, and the justice of his condemnation, and that he has no cause to think much that God rejects his services, and not give peace unto him.

After this, the sinner gives an account that he finds a spirit of love to God, sorrow for sin, aiming at the glory of God, hating of sin, etc. In this case he may be told:

1. That there is a great resemblance between common and saving grace. Common grace is the picture of sanctifying grace, and common affections are sometimes stronger than saving. Pharaoh justifies God, Saul weeps, one who was far from sincerity tells Christ that he will follow Him wherever He goes, the Jews cry *Hosanna to the Son of David,* the Israelites sang God's praise, but soon forgot His works.

2. That while they have such pangs of affection, it will be very hard for them to see their hypocrisy. Their fear of damnation makes them catch at any appearances of sincerity, and their pride makes them have a high opinion of their attainments. Men sometimes in that frame make such signs as do indeed show their hypocrisy to be arguments of their sincerity.

3. That it is a very dangerous thing for them to think that they are sincere while they are not. Then they will bless themselves when God curses them. Then they will continue quietly in a natural condition and neglect the means of conversion. And if they do not see the deceit quickly, there is danger that they may grow so hard-hearted that, if they do see it afterwards, they will not be the better for it.

4. That they may be satisfied from such things as these, that they do not love God sincerely whatever appearances there are, viz., that they never had a work of humiliation; and sincerity never forgoes that; that they never closed with Jesus Christ, and the heart is never purified without faith. All those affections that go before faith, let them be never so strong, are deceitful. The first good action that any man performs is to give entertainment to the gospel. Other things follow upon that.

SOMETIMES he gives an account that he believes on Jesus Christ. He does not trust in his own righteousness, but places his hope in Christ. In this case the minister may tell him that there is a great deal of faith that does not justify. Some believe for a time, Luke 8:13. *Some receive the Word with joy, and in a time of temptation fall away,* Matthew 13:20-21. *Some believed on Christ, but did not confess Him,* John 12:42. Several sorts of faith do not justify, as:

1. A historical faith. Men receive the history of the gospel for a truth, and take it for granted that Jesus Christ is the Son of God and Savior of the world, and if any should

deny it or dispute against it, they would be very zealous against him. It would stir up their indignation. If they have any workings of infidelity, yet they generally go with that persuasion that the gospel is true. But this is no more than a Turk will say about his religion. This historical faith dies not mortify men's corruptions, John 2:23-25. Many profane men have this historical faith.

2. A considerable confidence that Christ will save them. They are persuaded that they shall obtain salvation by Christ, and they rejoice in the hope of it. This confidence is a distinct thing from justifying faith. It is good or bad according to the grounds of it. Godly men have frequently such a confidence from the experience of a work of grace in their own hearts, and the manifestation of the love of God; but this is not justifying faith but a faith of assurance. Carnal men may have such a confidence arising from an imagination that God loves them and from an opinion of their own goodness. But this is not justifying faith, but presumption.

3. A dependence upon Christ on the encouragement of a man's own goodness. He hears the gospel, or has some common illumination discovering something of God's readiness to pardon sinners through Christ and, considering what he is, he ventures on Christ. When a man savingly believes, he ventures upon Christ upon gospel encouragements; but another ventures, being encouraged from the consideration of his prayers, tears, conscientiousness, or on that encouragement that he is not very bad. So he thinks such a one as he may venture; whereas, if he did see himself as bad as indeed he is, he would not venture on Christ. The man makes partly his own righteousness and partly the righteousness of Christ the foundation of his faith. He does not exclude the righteousness of Christ, but the preponderating consideration, and that which especially emboldens him to venture is his own righteousness. His own righteousness is the first foundation of his hope, though he

takes in the plea also of the righteousness of Christ. He sees enough in Christ for such a one as himself, but not for the worst of sinners.

But possibly he will plead for himself that he was much affected with Christ and with the mercy of God. It was more than ordinary; he never had such a light before. In this case he may be told that carnal men sometimes have superficial discoveries of Christ and are affected therewith, Matthew 13:20. Men have considerable enlightenings and tastes, yet may fall away; and it is no wonder they should be affected with the mercy of God. If men apprehend that God has pardoned them, they cannot but be affected with it. As pardon affects men, so does imaginary pardon.

He may further plead for himself that it was just so with him as it has been with godly men as he has heard them to express themselves; that all his objections were answered. He was backward before, but he had such a discovery of Christ that all his objections vanished away and he had nothing to say.

But he may be told that the reason why some men's objections are all answered is not from the greatness of the light that God gave them, but from the ignorance of their own hearts. They did not see so much of their own badness as thoroughly to feel the power of an objecting spirit. If they had seen how bad they were, their objections would not have been answered. A little matter will answer the objections of an ignorant and conceited man. They do not have enough light to make such strong objections as they would do if they knew themselves, and so all their objections are easily answered.

SOMETIMES he builds his confidence upon some particular Scriptures. One Scripture is I John 3:14, *We know that we are passed from death to life because we love the brethren.* He says he finds such a spirit in himself and he thinks his condition is good. But he may be told:

1. There is a great difference between loving the people of God for their piety and honoring them for their piety. Many natural men have some convictions that godly men are choice men and happy men; and, if they think a man is a sincere man, they honor him and have a respect for him. So Herod had respect for John, Mark 6:20, but these men do not have a sincere love to them for their piety. They do not love God nor godliness, therefore they do not love godly men for their piety.

2. There is a great difference between loving godly men for their piety and loving them for their morality. Godly men are moral men. Some of them are eminent for justice, sobriety, and faithfulness, and these are very lovely things in the eyes of many natural men. They love them upon that account, Daniel 6:3, 18. Darius had a great love for Daniel, but it was not upon the account of his piety, but his prudence and morality. Morality is lovely in the eyes of many carnal men. Some love godly men because they are related to them; some because they are friendly to them, and some because of their moral qualifications who do not have any love to them upon the account of their piety. The moral carriages of the people of God flow from a spirit of piety, but morality and piety are very different things, and some persons who have a love to them upon the account of their morality may have no love to them upon the account of their piety.

Another Scripture that he may build a confidence on is I John 5:11, *Whosoever believeth that Jesus is the Christ is born of God.* By this rule he says he is in a good condition. He believes this; therefore he is regenerate. In this case he may be told that the believing here spoken of is the receiving of it as certain upon the testimony of God. Many men have a common persuasion that Christ is the Son of God from tradition and from His miracles, which is in a more general acceptance called believing, John 2:23, and yet they are not born of God. But more properly they are said to believe it who receive it upon God's testimony, and those men who have only a common persuasion are indeed believers. They who do not have grace do not properly believe the Word of God.

Another Scripture that he takes notice of to strengthen his confidence is Matthew 5:6, *Blessed are they that hunger and thirst after righteousness.* His conscience testifies that he does so, therefore he hopes that he is blessed. In this case he may be told that, though some desires of grace are grace, yet all desires of grace are not grace as men may act hypocritically when they pretend to desire grace just as they may when they do desire grace. For:

1. Many carnal men desire grace. It is a common thing for ungodly men to desire grace, especially when terrified with the Word. They desire to be converted. Some men have lighter convictions and they have faint and anguishing desires, and some have more smart terrors and they think they would give all they have in the world to be converted. So it was with the foolish virgins, Matthew 25:8.

2. Desires of grace may arise from natural principles. Grace is not only desirable for its own sake, but there are several benefits that attend it which may make natural principles crave it. Grace is an honorable thing, Hebrews 11:2. It gains respect among men and procures a good name for men in the world. Hence, pride makes men crave it. Grace is a means of many outward blessings, 1 Timothy 4:8, and upon this account, men out of a selfish spirit may desire it. Grace is necessary in order to salvation, Hebrews 12:14, and upon this account, nature makes men crave it.

After he is delivered from his confident opinion of his good estate, and sees himself to be in a natural condition still, it may be needful upon that occasion:

1. To encourage him, for he is in danger to be too much cast down, so as to hinder his future diligence. He may be encouraged from the consideration of God's goodness in discovering that deceit which would have proved his bane.

He was in a dangerous way, but God has delivered him and so put him in a nearer capacity to be converted. God's not suffering him to continue in his delusion is a hopeful sign that God intends mercy to him. He is now under greater advantages than before, John 9:41.

2. To warn him that he does not run into the same error again; for he is still under the reigning power of a self-righteous spirit, and may get a false opinion of conversion again. Some strike upon that rock several times, therefore he must be cautioned not to be deceived with the appearances of grace, nor to give way to the flattery of his own heart. If he should take up such a persuasion again, it is doubtful that he would not be delivered. Relapses are dangerous and, if he should begin to think so, it would be best to advise with those that can inform him before he can be confirmed in such an opinion.

3. To lead him into the understanding of his own badness and insufficiency to help himself. This is an advantageous time to drive him out of himself and bring on the work of conversion. When he feels his own hypocrisy, the best way is to follow until he is quite emptied of himself. It is good policy to improve a victory and to help him to a thorough sight of himself so that he may be prepared for Christ.

SOMETIMES, after a man has been seeking for awhile and has passed through many changes, there is reason to fear that he will leave off. He has a great deal of discouragement. Others obtain and he is left. God does not make the Word powerful on his heart. He does not get forward and it may be perceived that he is more slightly than he was. In this case it is best:

1. To encourage him, for the discouragements that he is under are a great cause of apostasy. Therefore it is best to hearten him up. The notion of the giant-like stature of the Canaanites and the strength of their walls was a great

inducement to Israel to entertain thoughts of returning back to Egypt. So it is in this case and may be encouraged two ways.

(1) By showing the possibility of his obtaining mercy. So Caleb told the people that they were able to overcome and, if God delighted in them, he would bring them in. Thus he may be encouraged by showing him that God can help him and that nothing appears to how that God will not help him. His mercy is free; He has pardoned others as bad as he. His providences to him are consistent with designs of grace.

(2) By showing him the wonderful benefit that he will have if he does obtain mercy. Besides that peace and communion with God which he will have in this life, he will enjoy eternal salvation in the other world which is inconceivably great. It would be a great thing to have his punishments moderated, much more to be delivered from them. It would be a great thing to be saved out of hell after hundreds of years, greater to be preserved from going there. It would be a great thing to be kept out of hell and allowed to live a natural life always upon the earth, greater to be translated into the glorious presence of God and to be like the angels of God, always beholding the face of the Father. It is worth the while to go through any difficulty for heaven. Heaven will make amends for all. If the way to heaven were rocks and mountains, yet it is worth the while to travel there. The people of Israel were often told of the excellency of the land of Canaan, that it was a land flowing with milk and honey, and a land of vineyards and olive yards, wheat and barley. So it is useful to set before him the glorious happiness that the people of God will enjoy in another world.

2. To warn him of his danger, for security has a great hand in apostasy; to remind him what a miserable condition he would cast himself into if he should cast off fear and restrain prayer before God. Sometimes when men aposta-

tize, they fall into despair; and God suffers them to be miserably hurried and haunted by their own conscience, and no means can deliver them. So it was with Judas. Sometimes this shortens their days and does not allow them to continue in this world. When they draw back, God withdraws protection from them and they quickly die. When they neglect seeking eternal life, God denies temporal life to them; and sometimes He leaves them to be very wicked. They sometimes become of the number of the basest of men, 2 Peter 2:20-22; Matthew 12:44-45, and they are in dreadful danger of eternal fire, and that misery which no creature knows how to grapple with. Such considerations as these may help him against the sloth and slightness of his spirit.

Sometimes he complains he is followed with atheistical thoughts. He is frequently followed with questions about the being of God. In this case the minister may:

1. Acquaint him that, though this is a great sin, it may be forgiven. There is an abundance of atheism in the hearts of men. The lives of men show that they have much of this spirit, Titus 1:16, and many persons who have complained of this have afterwards been converted. Some who are godly men are much exercised with this temptation, Psalm 77:12-13. And, therefore, though he should not make light of it, yet he should not draw up any dark conclusions against the possibility of his salvation.

2. Convince him that there is a God, and settle his heart about that great truth.

(1) By evidencing to him the being of God, which he may do especially from the works of creation thus: the things which we see are made things. They are finite, compounded, corruptible and, therefore, it is impossible that they should be of themselves. That which is finite is not eternal but was made in time out of nothing. That which is compounded was compounded by some other thing. That which is corruptible does not have its being from itself. We

could not be of ourselves and, therefore, the first man who was of the same nature with us could not be of himself, and He that made these things must be an infinitely glorious God. He that could bring the world out of nothing, and make the creatures that are therein with wonderful variety of properties and virtues must be one of infinite perfection, that is, God, Romans 1:20, Psalm 19:1.

(2) By removing those objections that prove snares to him, if that is a snare to him that we do not see God. He may be told that we do not question many other things which we never saw. We do not doubt that there are such countries as France and Spain. Several things are invisible, such as the souls of men, angels, and devils (unless they assume a shape), yet we may be satisfied about these. There are other ways to satisfy us about the existence of things besides seeing them. We know some things by reason and some things by faith, Hebrews 11:3. If that is a temptation to him that others do not believe the being of God, he can plainly perceive by the lives of men that, whatever they pretend, they do not really think that there is a God. He may be told that, though they are not fully persuaded that there is a God, yet they cannot be fully persuaded that there is not a God. They have so much light they cannot extinguish it. There is not a perfect atheist in the world. Besides, carnal men are led by their corruptions and their reason is very much darkened, and there is no weight to be laid upon their thoughts. Shall we think there are no Antipodes because some ignorant men have denied it? Shall we question the roundness of the earth because some others think otherwise? We may not offer violence to our reason because of the sottishness of other men. If that is a snare to him, to conceive how God can be of Himself, how it is possible that He should be without being made, he may be told that, if that is above his reason to fathom, yet that is not contrary to reason as it is to think that a company of finite things should be of themselves. Besides, if there are beings, there

must of necessity be some first being. If the rest are made, yet there must be one that was not made. To say that nothing was made, and to say that all things are made, are equally absurd. Those things that are made could not have been unless there was something that was not made. Seeing many things have a being, there must be one being that is of himself. They could not interchangeably make one another, but there is one who was not made but is of himself, who is GOD.

SOMETIMES he complains that he is followed with horrible injections, blasphemous thoughts, and other wicked thoughts that are a great affliction to him and take away the comfort of his life. They make him a terror to himself. In this case he may be told:

1. That so far as they are injected by Satan, they are not imputed to him. The heart of man is very bad, and from that fountain of sin exceedingly wicked thoughts may arise; but when persons are violently followed with such thoughts, they are usually injected by Satan. They are some of his fiery darts spoken of in Ephesians 6:16. And when he casts them in, the man is no more guilty than he who hears a man blaspheme. If a man were perfectly holy, that could not prevent such injections if God let Satan loose upon him.

2. That his nature is so corrupted that those injections more or less taint him. The heart is like tinder, and these temptations will make some impression, though he has a detestation of those thoughts and labors against them. Yet there is a principle in the heart to fall in with them and, generally, upon such occasions, person contract guilt. And it is but rare, if ever, that men are merely passive at such a time. The sin that is in men easily besets them, Hebrews 12:1, and therefore it becomes him to be confessing before God the wretchedness of his own heart in favoring in any degree those temptations.

3. That such temptations are no sign that God does not

love him. He may not gather from this that God has given him up to Satan, for this has been the condition of some very godly men. This is an exercise that God has brought upon some who have been dear to him. As Satan is wont to tempt the best of men, so some of the choicest with these suggestions. This is not too great an affliction to be brought upon such men as God loves. The devil may, in this manner, hurry those who he shall not be able to destroy. Paul in likelihood had some such temptations, 2 Corinthians 12:7. God, for holy ends, may suffer those whom He loves to be thus exercised that they may learn their own weakness and be humbled before God.

4. That it is not very usual for God to suffer men to be long followed with these injections. Though there are some instances to the contrary, yet more ordinarily, after awhile, God restrains Satan, though no man can determine any precise time. Yet, after awhile, they are wont to be removed. God may so far hear prayers as to remove this affliction.

SOMETIMES he complains bitterly of the badness of his own heart and speaks of it as exceedingly bad. He says he never saw it so bad as of late, and seems to be almost discouraged thereby. In this case he may be told:

1. That the heart of the natural man is exceedingly bad. Many times, through restraints of corruption and common grace, the badness of it is hidden; but the heart of every natural man is desperately wicked, Jeremiah 17:9. Whatever appearances it may make, it is utterly corrupt; every sin is unmortified. Those sins that they have not been accustomed to, those sins that their tempers do not dispose them to, those sins of whose baseness they have the deepest sense and their hearts are totally empty of all goodness, there is not one spark of goodness in them. The principle of sin is as strong in them after they are enlightened and reformed as it ever was.

2. That it is necessary for him to be convinced of the

badness of his own heart. When men see the badness of their own hearts, they are ready to be discouraged; but they are then in a more hopeful condition than before. If men are strangers to their own hearts, they will trust in themselves and neglect Christ. God first reveals to them what they are and then He reveals the excellency of Christ to them. Men will never come to Christ until they are convinced what corrupt, blind, and dead creatures they are. And, therefore, the more God shows him of the badness of his heart, the more graciously He deals with him. The badness of the heart is a matter of sorrow, but the sight of that badness is a matter of encouragement. The more they see of that, the more hope there is of their being prepared for Christ.

3. That it is his best way to search his own heart farther. Many times, men will complain bitterly of the badness of their own hearts and, one time after another, give an account that they have seen more in their hearts than they ever did before, and yet are far from seeing what they must see in their own hearts. And while it is thus, they should be put upon to study their heart that they may see more of them. Persons are afraid to see their own hearts and are wont to strive against it, seeking to persuade themselves that they are better than indeed they are. It crosses their pride and their false hopes to see the badness of their own hearts. Therefore, there is a need to stir them up thereunto, and to tell them of what consequence it is. The sight of the heart is like the opening of a festered wound; it prepares men for healing. They should be put upon to search themselves and led into the way to do it. Particular things may be propounded to them to search after. This is a very natural thing, for the sincerity of their conversion has a great dependence upon the thorough knowledge of their hearts.

QUESTION. At this time, is it not best to urge him to believe on Christ, though he does not thoroughly understand the badness of his own heart?

ANSWER 1. It may not be amiss while he is in this condition to mind him that it is his duty to believe in Christ, and to set forth sometimes the excellency and sufficiency of Christ before him. It may be several ways beneficial to him. It may help him to take notice of the contrariety and opposition of his heart to this duty and lead him into a further understanding of the corruption of his nature. It may give some check to that spirit of self-righteousness that prevails in him and make him sensible of the necessity of the righteousness of Christ unto his justification. It may serve to encourage as to the possibility of his salvation, and convince him that he is capable of being brought into a state of salvation.

ANSWER 2. Yet there is no ground to hope that, until he thoroughly sees himself, he will accept the offer of the gospel. Men must first be humble before they will believe. Invitations to come to Christ will never be successful until men are driven out from their false refuges. They may hear the most powerful arguments with a great deal of evidence and affection, but they will not be obedient. Either they will be afraid to come to Christ or have one thing or another to object. They will be fearful because they see so much sin, or because they do not know that God means them, or they do not have the inward call of the gospel. Under some notion or another, they will not come, or else they will come in a presumptuous manner and pretend to believe when they do not indeed believe. Either they will be borne down with unbelief, or they will get a false faith.

SOMETIMES the man complains that he does not have encouraging Scriptures come to him and, therefore, he fears that he is not under the work of the Spirit. Other men have encouraging Scriptures brought to them and, therefore, God does not deal with him as with those he is wont to convert. In this case the minister may tell him:

1. That if he has supporting considerations cast into his

heart, that is sufficient. There is no necessity to have encouraging Scriptures to come with a great deal of power upon his heart. There is need of some supporting considerations to maintain a hope and to keep him from despair; and if the heart is but support with a hope that he may obtain at last, that is sufficient. God deals very variously with men. Some that have many encouraging Scriptures never do obtain mercy.

2. That if he does continue to wait upon God, he may have encouraging Scriptures come to him after awhile. God knows what he stands in need of, and does not tie up Himself to the same method as to the circumstances of the work. He uses a great deal of variety. Scarce two persons are carried on exactly after the same manner. Some have more encouragements towards the beginning, and others towards the latter end of the work.

SOMETIMES he says that, if he were sure to obtain, he could be willing to take any pains. Yes, though God should hold him waiting a long while, and he could be content to go through any anguish of spirit; but that which sinks his heart and makes him dull is that he is not certain of success. In this case he may be told by the minister:

1. That all who have obtained mercy have sought upon the encouragement that they might obtain mercy. They did not know what the issue of it would be. The possibility of it was that which bore up their hearts in using the means. They had some hope mingled with fear and, if they had not sought upon the encouragement of the possibility, they would certainly have gone without mercy. The sick man does not say he will not use the means unless he is certain of a cure. The merchant does not say that he will not send his ship to sea unless he is certain of a prosperous voyage. The husbandman does not say that he will not plow and sow his land unless he is certain of a good crop. Men must wait upon God, upon this encouragement, that they may

obtain mercy, John 2:8-9.

2. That the mere loss of their pains is a small matter. It will be a dreadful thing for a man to lose his soul; but the mere loss of their labors is a small matter. A man may well venture the loss of his labor in hope of the salvation of his soul. A man who is sick will venture the loss of a little expense for the preservation of his life. Men have no cause to be very scrupulous about the loss of their pains, the loss of their souls will be far sorer.

3. It is not fit that men should be sure to obtain mercy until they believe in Christ. There is security enough that, if they do believe in Christ, they shall be saved; and there is no reason that God should be desirous to make a new covenant and secure salvation to any other condition. God has descended low enough when He promises salvation to believing; and it is too much for any man to desire that God should promise it to praying, to reading, to reforming, etc. Especially seeing those things are done with a false heart, only for salvation.

4. If men are thoroughly scared with the danger of damnation, they will readily improve their possibility and not stand for assurance of success. Men will be glad of a possibility and not neglect the means because they have no more encouragement. If a man is cast into the sea, he will not neglect swimming because he is not certain that he can swim to the shore. If a man is pursued by an enemy, he will not stand still because he is not certain that he shall get clear. If men stand convinced of their dreadful danger in neglecting to seek, they will betake themselves to the use of means at a venture rather than run the hazard of their souls.

SOMETIMES he complains that, after he has told the minister how it is with him, it seems to him as if he had told a company of lies, and he is terrified with the apprehension of it. In this case he may be told:

1. That these thoughts rise partly from the frightfulness

of his conscience. He is in a terrified condition, and so the sound of a shaking leaf will scare him. He flees when no one pursues. He imagines dangers where there are none. He has a trembling, guilty conscience, and he is afraid that he sins when he does not, and is ready to charge things upon himself without cause.

2. That these thoughts arise from those contrary workings that are in his own heart. Sometimes he has a great sense of danger. Sometimes he has but a little sense of it. Sometimes he is afraid he has committed the unpardonable sin, and then he is not afraid of it. He has a great variety and change of frames and, whatever account he gives of the workings of his own heart, he has had some contrary workings thereunto. So that after he has told what workings of the heart he had, he has reflections because he remembers some contrary workings of heart.

SOMETIMES a man who has been seeking after peace with God a great while leaves off for some months together. He is followed with guilt and comes and makes his case known unto the minister. In this case it is very suitable:

1. To reprove him for his backsliding and set before him the sinfulness of what he has done, and the danger that he has exposed himself unto. He has quenched the Spirit, the tendency of whose motions was for his good. He has sinned against a great deal of light. When he was in a more hopeful way, he has relapsed into a sorrowful condition. He has lost ground and has a great deal of his work to do over again. God must be greatly provoked with him.

2. To encourage him, notwithstanding, by assuring him that he is capable of mercy. God invites backsliders to return to him. Persons are sometimes cured of relapses. God has mercy enough to pardon such sins; several persons have had experience of it. Sometimes the first attempt is not successful (as when David attempted to bring the ark into the

place prepared for it, but the next time he prospered).

3. To warn them that they do not do so again. They are in great danger because they have done so already. A beast that has once tired is more ready to do so again. Those temptations that have prevailed upon them are more likely to prevail again and, if they get a habit of backsliding, they will be the more incurable. Custom in an evil way naturalizes it to men; they run more readily into the same.

SOMETIMES a man goes on in a way of seeking a great while, yet seems to be at a standstill. The work does not go forward. He has the same fears, the same complaints, sets nothing further into his own heart. He is like a man with a chronic disease who, notwithstanding all medicines, continues much in the same posture. He is neither much worse nor much better; like a ship that beats upon the coast day by day and cannot get it. In this case the minister may:

1. Mind him that he may quickly die. The sense of approaching death is very terrifying and will stir men up to do their utmost. The face of death is terrible and, it may be, very profitable to work upon them; a sense that they may be quickly snatched away. They have the seeds of all diseases in them. God's judgments are as a light that goeth forth. Men are commonly snatched away before they are aware. Many of the Israelites that went out of Egypt did not live to go into Canaan. Their way is offensive to God and so He may take them away in His anger.

2. To convince them that they cannot make their own hearts better. One thing that makes men be at a stand is that they are waiting in expectation to mend their own hearts. They hope from Sabbath to Sabbath, and from one duty to another and, though they fail hitherto of their expectation, they find that afflictions do not do it, nor ordinances, nor mercies, nor examples. Yet they are promising themselves that, after awhile, they shall make them better, and it is fit

that they should be convinced of the impossibility of that. Their hoping and waiting for that is their snare. They may be showed how it is quite beyond their power. Whatever resolutions they take up, whatever pains they take, whatever encouragements, afflictions and terrors they have, yet it is beyond the compass of their power. They cannot understand the excellency of God and Christ, or the great evil of sin. Sin governs them and they cannot subdue it. Self-love may make them seek salvation but not love God above themselves. Men cannot be scared out of a sinful estate, though they may be scared out of some sinful practices.

3. To possess them that God is very angry with them, notwithstanding the pains they may take. For one great reason why they make no proficiency is because they live upon their duties. Though they do not think that their duties justify them, yet they pacify their consciences with them, and they think that God will have respect to the pains they take. They do what they can, and they do no more than some others, and they hope they stand upon better terms with God than formerly. And though they speak of their own badness, yet they imagine so much of their own goodness that they think it will be a hard case for God to damn them. Therefore, they should be convinced upon what terms they stand with God that, as there is no merit in their duties, so there is nothing to move God to pity them, nor to abate the anger of God towards them; but their best duties are provocations and imputed to them as sins.

SOMETIMES a man who has been in a very hopeful way quickly to get through the work of conversion, returns again to his old posture. He had, of late, great convictions of the badness of his own heart, the hypocrisy of his duties, the insufficiency of anything of his own to gain God's favor, and has such workings of heart as are wont immediately to procure submission to God and a work of humiliation. In a little time he tacks about and is as remote from humiliation as he used to be, as the children of Israel, when they were almost ready to enter into Canaan, fetched a compass and wandered a long time in the wilderness. In this case the minister may:

1. Warn him so that he is not afraid to see the badness of his own heart. Persons who have been praying for it are yet afraid of it when it comes to. It is such a doleful and uncomfortable spectacle that they cannot bear to behold it. The sense of it is so cross to their pride, and stirs up such fears of damnation, that they cannot tell how to do away with it, and labor to hide it from themselves and to get such affections as may comfort them. But they should be told that there is no cause for them to fear to see their own hearts, for it is dangerous to be ignorant of them, but not dangerous to see them. The sight of the heart is awful, but not hurtful. The heart is bad whether they see it or not, and they must see it before it is better. The surgeon must come to the bottom of the wound before he heals it.

2. Instruct him that there is a necessity of his submission to God; for his opposition to that has made him to quench those convictions of the Spirit which he had. He could not bear to yield himself a prisoner into the hands of God and to lie at his foot waiting for mercy, and that he has put him upon it to deliver himself from those convictions that led him away; but he must be instructed that there is a necessity of submitting himself to God. He cannot help himself, and God is bound to help him. God may leave him to perish if He will and, so long as he magnifies himself and refuses to resign up himself to God, God will not reveal Christ to him. He may pray, but he will not be heard; God resists the proud.

SOMETIMES he is afraid that his convictions are not like the convictions of other men, and he has several arguments to strengthen those fears.

One argument is that his convictions are only the workings of natural conscience and not from the Spirit of God. His convictions are the workings of his own thoughts; but he may be told that the way of the Spirit's working, when it does convince men, is by enlightening natural conscience. The Spirit does not work by giving a testimony, but by assisting natural conscience to do its work. Natural conscience is the instrument in the hand of God to accuse, condemn, terrify, and to urge to duty. The Spirit of God leads men into the consideration of their danger, and makes them to be affected therewith, Proverbs 20:27, *The spirit of man is the candle of the Lord, searching all the inward parts of the belly.* When men's own hearts are stirring them up to sin, and they have many reasonings about it, that is no sign that Satan is not busy with them. So when their own hearts are accusing and frightening of them, it is no sign that the Spirit of God is not at work with them. All the regular actions of conscience, all those convictions that are according to the Word of God are from the Spirit of God.

Another argument is that his terrors are not as great as other men's. Many others have such terrors that they are swallowed up therewith, almost distracted, and the town may take notice of it; but his terrors are more moderate by far. But he may be told that there is great diversity in the degrees of men's trouble so as to make him strive earnestly after salvation and do what he can do in order to it; so much as to make him thoroughly to reform, and earnestly to strive to get into a converted condition. Every ship that performs its voyage must have so much wind as may make the ship sail; but some ships have stronger and more tempestuous winds than others have. Some men are of a more tender spirit and less will prevail upon them than upon others; and some men, whose troubles are but small at the beginning, afterwards grow to a great height. God uses His sovereignty very much as to the degrees of men's trouble.

Another argument is that his terror did not begin as other men's did. Many others have been smitten in the preaching of the Word. The Word of God has been like a sharp sword in their heart; but his troubles came from the examples of others, or from some affliction, or from his fall into some sin.

But he may be told that other men never see the great evil of sin until they are converted. Men may see a moral evil in sin, and a great deal of the vanity and folly of it, though they are not under a preparatory work of the Spirit; but they never come to see the great evil of sin until they are converted. Men do not have a spiritual understanding given them until they are converted. As long as they remain under the preparatory work of the Spirit, no such things can be expected from them as are peculiar to saints. When once men come to see the evil of sin, they also see the glory of God. They mortify their sins and are brought into a state of sanctification.

Another argument is because he does not prosper in his seekings. He has been seeking a long time, and yet God stands at a distance from him. Other men get through it quickly. Some who began a long time since him have obtained peace with God, but he is left yet in a deplorable condition; but he may be told:

That it is a common thing with God to convert some in a far shorter time than others. One ship may spend twice as much time as another in performing the same voyage. One man's disease may be broke in far less time than another man's. Some men have more temptations and hindrances than others. The Spirit pursues some men more closely than others, and those that are longer under the work may be as soundly converted at last. The great reason why men do not hitherto prosper in their seekings is not that their first troubles were not like the troubles of other men, but because they trust in their own righteousness, and are not yet convinced of their own helpless condition and the badness of their own hearts.

QUESTION. But are not some men's convictions and terrors saving? Is there not a difference all along in the terrors of them that are elect and them that are reprobate?

ANSWER. There is no difference for a great while between the strivings of the Spirit in those that shall be converted and in those that shall not. As there may be no difference in the voyages of two ships for a pretty while, one of which at last arrives in the harbor, and the other is cast away, so it is here. Those that shall never be converted may have the same experiences for a considerable time that those have who shall be converted. There may be no differences in their awakenings, in their reformations, in their temptations, in their encouragements, nor in respect of their frames. This appears:

1. Because those strivings that men may have who shall never be converted are sufficient to bring men forward towards Christ. There is no necessity at all that the elect should have any other strivings, for a time, than what are common to reprobates. The convictions that reprobates may have are sufficient to bring men forward towards Christ. Those terrors that reprobates may have are sufficient to wean them from the world, to make them reform their lives and labor to be converted. If men have but such a sense of hell as many reprobates have had, there is no danger but they will take pains to be saved, Psalm 78:34. Though this will not convert them, yet it will bring them nearer to the kingdom of God than they were. It will make them travel towards Christ, and overcome several impediments that lay in the way of their conversion. Though they do not see the great evil of sin, yet they will be afraid of it. Though they do not see the excellency of holiness, yet they will seek after it. Common convictions are a preparation for conversion.

2. They who are converted are not capable of any strivings of the Spirit, but what are common until they come to be humbled and to believe. It is a pretty while after

God begins to strive with the elect, before they come to be humbled, and to believe in Christ; and before that, they are not capable of any strivings but what are common. What can there be but what is common to other men? Other men have fears of hell and judgment, sense of wrath, moral convictions of the evil of sin, encouragements, many discoveries of vileness in their own hearts, and deceitfulness. And what more can these have before they are humbled? They are not capable yet to see the evil of sin, the excellency of Christ, nor of godly sorrow, nor of sincere desires, because they are not converted. Why may not a reprobate have as much conviction as they? What are they capable of in their present circumstances but what many have had who are now in hell? Some speak of a saving conviction and contrition. What is it? If it is only of hell and wrath, reprobates have such as well as they. It cannot be the great evil of sin, for none can see that, but they are converted. Natural men are blind, Revelation 3:17.

3. If there is a difference, men might be able to tell what the difference is and apply it. There is a difference between common grace and saving grace, and we are able to give an account what it is. So if there was a difference between the convictions of the elect and reprobate, we might be able from the Word of God to tell what the difference is. If ordinary men could not do it, yet it might be expected that such as have a deeper insight into the Scriptures should. There God gives us rules to discern the difference that is in His dispensations; but no man in the world is able to tell what convictions of wrath and hell are peculiar to elect sinners and what are peculiar to reprobates. Can we distinguish them by their kinds, by their degree, by their continuance, by their immediate effects? What rules have we to guide us in this matter? And can we make an application to persons? If sinners give us a true account of their terrors, can we tell one that his convictions are such as are proper to the elect, and they will end in conversion, and another, that his

convictions are the convictions of reprobates, and that they will end in damnation? This would be a bold undertaking of any man. The Scripture is silent about it. Yes, the Scripture speaks the contrary, Luke 11:52, *them that were entering in ye hindered.*

SOMETIMES the man is afraid he shall die quickly, and lives in a great deal of torment upon that account. He is in anguish of spirit. This frame arises either merely from his sense of God's anger (he thinks God will immediately pour out His wrath), or sometimes besides this, there is something in providence that looks that way, or some word comes to him that makes him fear it such as "Set your house in order, for you shall die and not live." In this case, he should be told by the minister:

1. That he ought not to take up such a conclusion. No man should believe anything that may be false. He has no sufficient grounds to draw up any such peremptory conclusion, for the thing itself is uncertain. God's anger does not show it. God has been angry with him a long time, yet he lives. Neither do those other signs show that it shall be; such things have oftentimes failed.

2. That it is not usual with God to take men away when they are under earnest endeavors to be converted. God threatens sinners to take them away in the time of their security, when they say "peace, peace," 1 Thessalonians 5:3, Matthew 24:48. Though sometimes men die who are seeking after peace with God and, to all appearance, have not yet found, yet this is not an ordinary dispensation. When He is striving by His Spirit to bring them to repentance, it is a hopeful sign that God will wait awhile upon them. If we knock at a man's door, and they are all fast asleep and do not stir to open the door, we are wont to go away; but if we perceive that they are rising and preparing to open the door, we are content to wait awhile. God generally stays to see what work men will make of it.

3. That he has indeed no certainty of his life; his body is mortal and frail, and many men die suddenly. God has been much provoked by him and may justly snatch him away by a sudden stroke. Many times men have very little warning of death; the fear of death is of great use to forward the work of conversion. If men put far away the evil day, they thereby harden their hearts. The right numbering of their days is a means to make them apply their hearts to wisdom, Psalm 90:12. Upon this account it is good to nourish awful fears of death. Those make men sensible of the vanity of the world, of the dangerousness of sin, of the necessity of making haste to be converted. Therefore, ministers should say nothing to persuade them they are in no danger, for they are in real danger, and it is best for them to have the sense of it. This will solemnize their spirits and quicken them to their work. When afraid of death, they will be willing to take pains and not be hindered by temptations.

SOMETIMES he complains that he finds a dreadful murmuring spirit. He is dreadfully apt to quarrel with God, and cannot tell him how to justify him. It is a great terror to him, yet he cannot deliver himself from it. In this case he may be told:
1. That it is generally so with men under the work of preparation. There is scarce any but has experience of it. Men can hardly bear outward afflictions, much less appearances of damnation. When awakened sinners are called upon to submit to God, yield themselves prisoners to Him, there are two courses that men take to avoid it. One is to establish a righteousness of their own. They strive to pacify the anger of God; they would fain do something to engage the heart of God to save them. Upon that account they pray affectionately; they strive to make their hearts better. The other way is, when they find that their danger continues, after all their pains, they quarrel with God, object against His dispensations, and find fault with Him. They are in a

tumult; their hearts are in an uproar and they are murmuring against God's dealings.

2. That he may see much of his own heart in these murmurings. And indeed, these murmurings are a great occasion sometimes to bring men off from their own righteousness. Therefore it is good to lead him on this occasion into the sense of the wretchedness of his own heart. He may see in these workings much of his own hypocrisy. He has owned, many times, the need he has of free mercy and that he deserved condemnation. Yet now he murmurs as if God owed salvation to him. He may see much of the pride of his own heart in rising up against God, and of his boldness, and of his enmity to God. These workings of heart reveal a dreadful fountain of sin within.

That these objections which his heart makes against God's proceedings are causeless. He may be shown particularly that the ways of God are righteous, and that men have no reason to murmur against Him. It should be cleared up to him that God has great cause to find fault with him, but he has no cause to find fault with God.

Perhaps the man will object and say that men are brought under a necessity of sinning and yet are punished for sin. He will object that sin is decreed and cannot but be committed, yet it is punished. He may be told:

1. That the decree of God does not at all infringe the liberty of man. Though the decrees bring a necessity, yet men act as freely as if there were no decrees. The decree of God offers no violence to the will of man. Men choose the ways of sin, Isaiah 66:3, and therefore the decree is no excuse for sin. Men do not accept it when any wrong is done unto them, neither will God accept it as an excuse. Men act their own pleasure and dispositions when they sin. The necessity rising from the decree does not take away the commendableness of good actions, nor the blameableness of bad actions. This necessity does not cut off all rewards

and punishments.

2. That in this decree, God only uses His sovereign liberty. If God will make a multitude of men and angels, must He be bound to bring them all to eternal life? Who shall lay a prohibition upon God, that He shall not make use of some of them for the glory of His justice? If it is injurious for God to decree that men shall sin and then punish them for their sin, then He is utterly cut off from all opportunity for the glorifying of His justice; but it is worth the while for men and angels to suffer for the manifestation of God's vindictive justice.

If the man objects that the sin of Adam is imputed to him and, upon that account, he is deprived of original holiness, whereas he was not at all active in it and gave no consent to it, he may be told:

1. That men in many cases have a power to appoint others to represent them; and they are accordingly bound to stand or fall according to the carriage of representatives. Yes, men have a power to make representatives for others. These things are common in matters of a civil nature. Why, then, may not God, who has more power over men than they have over themselves, appoint one to represent them, to act on their behalf, according to whose carriage they should stand or fall?

2. That this was a fair and probable way for the good of mankind. It was as hopeful a way as for every man to stand by himself. There was less likelihood that all Adam's posterity should stand than that he should stand, only from the personal qualifications of Adam, which were certainly greater than his posterity would have had in the time of their childhood; but because Adam was under an exceedingly great bond, he had a great charge upon him, the happiness of all his posterity having a great dependence upon his carriage. Adam not only had the care of his own soul upon him, but he stood entrusted for many millions who

were to descend from him, and it was probable that this consideration should make him more careful to keep God's covenant.

3. If the man objects against the severity of God's law that punishes men with everlasting damnation, he may be told:

(1) It is very meet that He should appoint such a punishment that might be a great restraint to man's sinning. If God has appointed some little punishment, men would have been more bold to break the law of God. Experience shows that this severe punishment is not sufficient to keep multitudes from living in a way of sin. If the punishment had been less, men would have regarded it but very little.

(2) It was very meet that God should appoint a punishment that was suitable for the vindication of His great name. God loves Himself and His name is dear to Him, and it becomes God to annex such a penalty to His law as that His great name might be vindicated. God is a great God and, therefore, sin is a great evil; and it is very fit that if sin is punished, there is a punishment appointed some ways proportionable to the great evil of sin.

(3) That by God's appointing so dreadful a punishment, He makes no man miserable. God holds out the point of a sword; this will do them no harm if they do not run against it. God makes a dreadful pit; this will hurt no man if he does not run into it. God's law makes no man miserable; they make themselves miserable and are cruel to their own souls when they sin against Him.

(4) The punishment appointed for sin is no greater than the recompense of obedience. There is an equality in the law. The law is as bountiful to the obedient as it is severe to the disobedient. If the law appointed little rewards of obedience, and great punishments of disobedience, men would have more show for their complaints; but the reward is as great as the punishment. Heaven is as good as hell is bad.

If he objects that God has showed mercy to others who have not taken so much pains as he, that God pardons and gives grace to others but denies him, he may be told:

1. That his labor and service lays no bond upon God to show mercy to him. Whatever he has pretended in his prayers, he has no true regard to the glory of God. He has minded nothing lighter than his own salvation. He has been serving himself and not God. God is no ways obliged to give him such a reward. He has not merited grace, but has merited condemnation by such services. There is nothing in such services to work upon the mercy of God. God's mercy is not moved by any external thing. There is nothing in those services to engage the justice of God, they are far from being meritorious. There is nothing to engage the faithfulness of God. God has made no absolute promises to any hypocritical prayers.

2. That God has a liberty to bestow His grace upon whom He will. Mercy is God's own, and He will make choice who shall be the subjects of it. God is master of His own gifts; He will bestow them upon one and deny them to others. It is just for God to deny all sinners saving mercy, but if He pleases to have mercy upon some, none may prescribe who they shall be; but He may choose one and refuse another, 1 Corinthians 4:7.

3. That God never did bestow saving mercy upon any sinner while he quarreled against His proceeding. Before ever others had mercy, their spirits were brought down and they were brought to justify God and lie at His feet. If they had stood it out as He does, they would have gone without saving mercy, Isaiah 45:23, *To me every knee shall bow.*

If he objects that he has done what he can and yet God denies grace to him, that he gave way to a sluggish spirit and carried himself viciously; but he does what he can and what? Would God have more? He may be told:

1. That if he does what he can, he may not challenge

mercy from this. By what law will he demand saving grace because of that? That does not, in its own nature, take away God's liberty and His sovereignty; there is no wrong done him if God sees cause to deny him. Neither is there any promise whereby God has obliged Himself to those who do all they can. God has left it in His own liberty to deny them if He pleases.

2. That he does not do what he can. It may be he is, otherwise, very faulty, but however he does not do what he can because he does not own the sovereignty of God. He does not justify God, nor acknowledge that God may justly reject him after all. Indeed, he cannot do this without help from God, so he cannot pray and reform without assistance. Yet this is a thing he can do. Principles of nature may produce this effect. Many natural men have come to this. Men who have no natural principle have resigned themselves up to God, "their mouths have been stopped and they have become guilty before God."

If he objects that God requires him to believe whereas it is not in his power, that he is dead in sin and yet God binds him to believe and calls on him to believe, this seems very strange and hard. He may be told:

1. That though he has lost his power to obey, yet God has not lost His power to command. If he has lost his strength, yet God has not lost His authority. If a servant makes himself drunk and is not able to do his master's business, that is no excuse. God gave man power at first, and his prodigality does not deliver him from God's authority.

2. That in this way, God is pleased, many times, to work faith. Men are able to do many things in order to believe, and hereby they are put upon to prepare for that; and, in that way, many have had faith wrought in them. There have multitudes, by the blessing of God on the preaching of the gospel, been brought to embrace Jesus Christ.

SOMETIMES the man says he is afraid to do anything in religion, for whatever he does he is ready to trust to it. If he prays, fasts, reads, especially when he does those things with any affection, so he trusts in his conscientiousness. In this case he may be told:

1. That he may not neglect his duty by any means. He must be sure to attend his duty whatever ill use his heart is ready to make of it. He must not scare himself off from his duty because he is ready to trust in it. Duty must be done, God's command must be attended, whatever is the consequence of it. Men may not take upon them to judge when it is best to attend God's command, and when it is dangerous, and so give themselves a dispensation from their duty. As men must not do evil that good may come of it, so they may not neglect good lest evil come of that. Men must do their duty and run the adventure of their heart's making a bad use thereof.

2. That there is no necessity of men's trusting what they do. If God does but open their eyes to see the plague of their own heart, they will not trust what they do. When men are thoroughly convinced of the abominations that are in their hearts, and see the hypocrisy and formality of their duties, it is impossible they should trust in them. Their confidence in their duties rises from the opinion that they have of them, and when they come to understand the wretchedness of them, their heart will not gather confidence, but fear of them. And, therefore, it is their duty to study their own hearts, and labor to find out the wickedness of them.

When the man is told that there is a necessity of seeing his own heart in order to his humiliation, sometimes he objects that he is blind and cannot see. How can a blind man see his own heart? He may be told:

1. That he is indeed spiritually blind and, therefore, he cannot see the evil of sin. That is not to be seen until men have received a spiritual understanding from God and,

accordingly, there is no necessity of seeing that in order to his humiliation.

2. But yet he is capable to have an experimental sight of the badness of his own heart. Natural conscience is able to discern that. Men may find by experience that they are under the power of pride, of discontent, and carnal affection; and that they are utterly destitute of any love to God, or any gracious disposition. These things are not discerned by a spiritual eye but by a natural eye. Natural men may observe and discern the workings of their own hearts, Romans 7:8, *Sin taking occasion by the commandment, wrought in me all manner of concupiscence.*

SOMETIMES the man says he is willing to believe in Christ, but finds himself unable. He would be glad if he could believe, but it is beyond him. In this case he may be told:

1. That there is a mighty opposition in the heart of a natural man to believing in Christ. As it is with all other spiritual duties, so it is with this. Men do not love to believe in Christ, but have a contrariety thereunto, John 5:40, Matthew 23:37. The opposition rises partly from pride. They would rather be saved by their own works that they may have something to glory in. It is very cross to their haughty spirit to go out of themselves and be beholding to Christ alone for salvation, to have nothing of their own to glory in. Men do not love to see themselves as nothing; and partly it rises from fear. It seems to them a terrible thing to adventure upon Christ. They are not certain that God is free to accept them. They are not certain whether Christ's righteousness is sufficient for them. They do not see the encouragement that is in the gospel, and think it an unlikely thing that they shall be safe in such a way. Hence they have a trembling in their heart. Looking upon it as too great an adventure, they fear it will be looked upon as presumption, and that instead of mending their condition, they shall make

it worse. They should be afraid to stay away from Christ, but they are afraid to come to Him and, therefore, are not willing.

2. If the man was willing, what keeps him from Christ? The difficulty lies in the will. If the will is conquered, the man is conquered. Yes, faith in Christ is an act of the will. Faith is a choosing of Christ for his Savior. Christ is offered to men, and many encouragements are presented before them and, when once the will is gained to accept the offer, the man does believe on Christ. If men were willing, the difficulty would be at an end. They cannot be willing until they are able. They are not willing until the will is strengthened to comply with God's call.

3. That seeming willingness that is in many men is but feigned. They pretend a willingness to quiet their consciences. They do not, it may be, feel much opposition, but they are not, indeed, willing. They are willing to be saved, and willing to be saved by Christ rather than not be saved at all, and have some selfish desires that they could come to Christ, but there is no sincerity in them.

SOMETIMES the man says that he would fain submit to the will of God but cannot tell how. He has been striving after it a great while, but cannot attain it. In this case he may be told that natural men never sincerely strive after submission to God. They strive to submit after a fashion, and pray that they may, because they may hear that it is necessary in order to conversion, but they are never sincere in it. They do it in a false and deceitful way, which appears:

1. Because they are laboring to make their hearts better. They are laboring to mend themselves and, upon this account, they labor after it that they may not be necessitated to submit to the will of God; that their own goodness may be a bond upon God to save them, that it may not be in the free liberty of God to do what He pleases with them and, upon this account, they strive to submit to God that they

may make a righteousness of that.

2. Because at the same time they are hiding their own hearts from themselves, they are afraid to see how bad they are. If they have any convictions of their own badness, they will stifle them if they can. They are laboring to excuse themselves, and love to look upon anything in themselves that seems like goodness. They are persuading themselves that they are better than they are, which is a great hindrance to submission.

3. Because they are not thoroughly convinced of a necessity of submission to God. If they were convinced of a necessity of it, they would do it; and if they are not convinced of it, they cannot strive sincerely after it. As long as men hope that they will make a shift without it, they will not heartily seek after it. As long as men hope that their own righteousness will lay a bond upon God, and that it is not fair for God to condemn them, they will not heartily endeavor after submission.

When men are called upon to submit to God and resign themselves to His sovereignty, they say they do so. They cannot help themselves, but must justify God. In this case, there is great need to examine whether their submission is of the right kind; for there is a show of submission, which is not real humiliation, and there are these signs of a false submission.

1. When it is the fruit of their own strivings. Men hear that they must submit themselves to God before they obtain mercy; and they strive accordingly for it and work up a kind of image of submission to God. They bring themselves to own that they are in God's hands, and He may do what He will with them. This is never right. When men are brought to submit to God, indeed, the thing is forced by the power of conviction. They strive against it, but were so evidently convinced of the insufficiency of themselves and the justice of God that they had no other way left them but to fall into the hands of God as it was with those lepers,

2 Kings 7:4.

   2. When men make a righteousness of their own submission. When men have a false submission, they are wont
to be proud of that, and to think that God will be taken with
them. They look upon it as a choice frame of spirit, and rejoice in it as a thing pleasing to God; but when men indeed
submit to God, they see nothing in it to be proud of. They
see themselves all over defiled like lepers, empty of all
good, and look upon this submission as having nothing at
all of goodness in it. They see they are merely forced to it,
that they have no other way to take, but to fall into the
hands of the living God.

   3. When, notwithstanding their submission, they are
still striving to make their hearts better. If you ask them
whether they are striving to love God, and to do duties for
His glory, they say, "Yes." They are laboring after it. You
may be sure they do not submit to God, but are laboring to
get some goodness of their own to commend them to God;
they are not sensible of their own impotency. But if a man
indeed submits to God, he sees himself dead in trespasses
and sins. Ask him whether he is striving to make his heart
better. He will say he can easily remove a mountain as do
it; that he has been striving after it a great while, but now
he finds that he has no power. His heart is as dead as a
stone. There is no disposition to anything that is good in
him. It is quite out of his reach. If God does not make him
better, it will never be affected.

   4. When men say they have been brought to that many a
time. When some men are inquired of as to whether they
were brought to submit to God's sovereignty, they say,
"Yes, many a time." Sinners in trouble of conscience say it
has been so oftentimes with them. This shows it is not a
right submission. Godly men, after their conversion, may
submit many times to God, but that submission differs
much from this. That is a gracious submission, and they do
not see at the same time themselves utterly destitute of all

grace; but that submission that goes before the closing with Christ is never wrought any more than once. When it is wrought, it may continue some little time until God reveals Christ to a man; but this work is never wrought over and over again in the soul.

5. When men are afraid they are not humbled enough. Some men who pretend to submission, as afraid that they are not humbled enough, and they wish they may be humbled more, this makes it evident that they do not indeed submit, it is a sign that they make a righteousness of their submission. When men indeed submit to God, they are never exercised with any such scruples, because they do not look upon their submission as a thing that commends them to God. When a man submits, he absolutely resigns himself up as a prisoner to God, is wholly broken off from his own righteousness and sufficiency, and leaves himself with God and does not do it under a notion that there is any excellency in it, but out of necessity leaves himself with God.

6. When men submit to God as looking upon Him as not being very angry. Some sinners submit to God and, at the same time, think they have some love to God and some care for His glory; and, accordingly, they look upon their peace half made. Truly, this is no difficult matter. It is easy for a man to put his life into the hands of his friend. There is no great opposition to submit to God when a man is pretty confident that God will save him; but it is another thing to submit to God when a man does not see a spark of goodness in himself, when he looks upon God as bitterly angry with him, and is much afraid that God will utterly destroy him. When men submit under such circumstances, it is evident that God has conquered them and that their wills are broken.

QUESTION. What is to be said to a man in case he should say that he is willing to be damned?

ANSWER 1. No man acting understandingly is willing

to be damned. All ungodly men do interpretatively love damnation, Proverbs 8:35, but no man who understands himself is willing to be damned. It is against nature. Nature teaches every man to desire happiness. Damnation is a dreadful terror to those who know what it is, Isaiah 33:14.

ANSWER 2. No such thing is required of men. For God has put a spirit of self-love into men and binds them to love themselves, and commands men to be seeking of salvation, John 6:27, Luke 13:24.

Such willingness is either only pretended; or, if real, it must arise either from desperate rage and passion, or from some violent pang of false affection to God. The Spirit of God does not stir up such workings in the hearts of men.

SOMETIMES a sinner inquires how he may come to know his own heart. He is told that it is needful for him to know it, and inquires what he should do in order to it. In this case he may be directed to these three ways:

1. To observe the sinful workings of his own heart. The hearts of men are often working in a way of pride, discontent, worldliness, envy, etc. And, by observing these, a man may learn an abundance of the badness of his own heart, if he considers with himself how far such a spirit would carry him if God did not restrain it. As when a man sees the fire burn the wood on the hearth, he gathers that it would consume the house too if not restrained.

2. To examine those shows of goodness that the heart makes. The heart makes many shows of goodness sometimes of sorrow for sin, of love to God, to godly people, of love to ordinances, of desires to be converted, of believing the Word of God, of humility, of patience, of thankfulness; and the way to know the heart is to search whether it is not false in these appearances, to examine the ends and motions of those frames and workings of heart, whether the root of them is not self-love, fear of hell, hope of merit, etc.

3. To try his heart by supposing some suitable cases to

it. He may suppose to himself that such godly men as he pretends love to should slight and despise him; that God should take away such a child from him, that God should convert some others and leave him under guilt and terrors; that his estate should be lost that there should come persecuting times; that he were in the hands of enemies that would kill him if he would not carry on sinfully; that God should not come to take away his life before he is converted. By questioning seriously with himself what he thinks he should do in such cases, he may come to have more understandings in his own heart. Changes of condition make great discoveries of the heart, and supposed changes sometimes do a good deal that way. Such questions, if seriously considered, may be as touchstones to reveal what is in the heart. The answer of the heart to such inquiries, may give men a great deal of light to see themselves by.

QUESTION. How does God show men the badness of their own hearts?

ANSWER 1. The means whereby God effects it is by leading men into temptation. Men in continuance of time fall into temptation and so the mask falls off from their hearts, and they come to have an understanding of the plague that is therein. Sometimes, by some reason of some temptation, they are drawn into some moral evil, and that reveals their hypocrisy and corruption. Sometimes, temptations prevail upon them to make them worldly and proud. Sometimes, by afflictions, the discontentment of their hearts is stirred up. So by God's not hearing their prayers, by converting other persons, sometimes by hearing the doctrine of God's sovereignty, or the strictness of the law. Sometimes the Word of God and sometimes the works of God are a temptation to them, and occasion them to be dead to that which is good and make their corruptions work violently, Romans 7:8, *Sin taking occasion by the command-*

ment, wrought in me all manner of concupiscence.

2. As to the manner, it is done gradually. God does not lead men at once into an understanding of their hearts; as the surgeon, by degrees, comes to the bottom of the sore. God could, at once, make men see the bottom of their own hearts, as when the jailer was converted; but, in this way, men would not have such experience of the deceitful turnings and windings of their own hearts. But He generally shows it to them by degrees, and they are a long while before they come to an understanding of them. They see something of their hearts and then grow into a pretty good opinion of them again; they have many partial discoveries of their heart. Sometimes, they go forward in discerning their hearts, and then go backward again. They get ground and then they lose it. They seem as if they would presently come to an understanding of them, and then there is a stop put to it for a pretty while. A great deal of time is consumed before they come to have a thorough understanding of themselves. Men are sometimes years under trouble before they attain unto it.

QUESTION. What must men know of their own hearts before they are converted?

ANSWER. In general, they must know so much as is sufficient to bring them off from trusting in their own righteousness and their own strength. Some men know a great deal more of their own hearts than other men. They see many particular deceits and workings of corruption that other men do not see, and no man knows his heart so before conversion but he may learn a great deal more after he is converted. But so much must be known by every man as is sufficient to break him off from trusting in himself. It is the sight of his own heart that takes him off from trusting in himself. Let him hear never so much about the insufficiency of his own righteousness, he will trust in himself until he sees his own heart. But when he sees that thoroughly, it is impossible he should trust in himself, for he sees there is nothing there to trust in. Particularly:

1. He must see himself under the reigning power of sin. If men imagine that they have no great disposition to sin, or that their corruptions are in any degree mortified, they will commend themselves to God upon that account, and will not see it just and fair for God to condemn them. There is no absolute necessity that they should have the particular consideration of every corruption that is in their hearts; but they must see that they are under the dominion of sin, that a spirit of self-love reigns in them, and that their heart is contrary to that which is good. They find such workings of pride, discontentment, and enmity to Christ as shows to them they have abominable hearts; that their hearts are like the hearts of devils, as full of sin as a toad is full of poison, Romans 7:9.

2. To be empty of all goodness. He has no inclination to anything that is good, that there is no disposition to that which is good, but a total emptiness. It may be he does not think particularly of every grace that he is destitute of that, but sees that he is utterly void of spiritual life, that he has no power to do any good. He is dead in sin, wretched and miserable, and poor, blind, and naked. Before that, he was convinced of a weakness, but now he finds himself dead. He thought before that he had little strength, now he sees that he has none. There is not one spark of goodness in him, nor any power to get any. He is stripped of all his perfections and sees an utter emptiness in himself of all that good. He has no love, no godly sorrow, no thankfulness, no humility, no spiritual desires. Those appearances that he had are all vanished out of sight. He cannot do anything. There is no seed of any goodness in him. If he is advantaged with all manner of helps, yet is quite beyond his power to work up any good frame in his heart. He prays, but there is no goodness in his prayers, and he is incapable of working up any. He is not in a swoon, rubbing and chafing will not

fetch him to life, but he is everlastingly dead in sin unless
God will put a principle of life into him.

SOMETIMES the man says that he sees that he can do
nothing of himself. In this case he may be told that the best
saint in the world can do nothing of himself, John 15:4.
Those who do a great deal for God, and have a gracious
principle, still know that they can do nothing of themselves;
and a natural man may stand convinced of this, that he can
do nothing of himself, though he is very proud and imagines that he does God a great deal of choice service. When
he says that he can do nothing of himself, he only means
that he can do nothing without assistance from God. This a
man may see and yet be a great stranger to his own heart.
The thing that he wants to see is that he has no principle of
doing any good, that there is no power nor inclination in
him, but that he is totally and everlastingly dead in sin, unless God infuses a new principle into him.

SOMETIMES men have great discoveries of their own
heart for a good while together, and yet do not come to lie
at God's foot. They say themselves that they cannot do it.
In this case he may be told:
    1. That they cannot deliver themselves; that it is utterly
impossible for them to mend their own hearts. Men may see
themselves bad and insufficient, yet not be brought to despair as to their own power; be nourishing a secret hope
that in time, with some advantages, their heart will be
brought to a better pass. Therefore, it is best to possess
them with a sense of their utter insufficiency to help themselves. They may as well make a world as make their own
hearts good. They cannot work faith in themselves, John
6:44.
    2. That they cannot deserve that God should give grace
to them. They cannot force God to work regeneration in
them; they have no natural excellency to engage God. They

cannot work the mercy of God, nor engage the justice of God to save them. God is not bound to them to help them. There is nothing to hinder Him if He pleases; there is nothing to oblige Him, they cannot compel God. God is free to help them or deny them help as it pleases Him.

3. That it is dangerous to stand it out against God. If they do not yield, they are in danger either to be left of God to a senseless spirit, or to get a false confidence, or to be snatched away out of the world. Men stand in slippery places who continue to be stubborn against great conviction. It is not long before the scale will turn. If they do not quickly submit, there is danger of their rejection.

SOMETIMES the man says that now he can justify God, however He deals with him, and yet it is evident that he is not brought off from his own righteousness. In this case he may be told:

1. That he must beware that he does not make a righteousness of this. Pride will feed upon any appearance of good qualifications, and if he lots upon it that now his heart is better than it was, and that God is taken with him, he will greatly deceive himself. His justifying of God is no justification of himself. His justifying of God will not make God to justify him. Though he justifies God, yet God condemns Him.

2. That some men do justify God from a partial conviction of the righteousness of their condemnation. Conscience takes notice of their sinfulness and tells them they may righteously be damned, as Pharaoh who justified God, Exodus 9:27. And they give some kind of consent to it, but many times it does not continue. They have only a pang upon them that usually dies away after a little time. This justifying of God differs much from that which immediately goes before conversion, which is a fixed and thorough conviction arising from a thorough understanding of their own hearts.

SOMETIMES the man seems to be upon the very borders of despair. For some men are nearer to it a great deal than others, he is in anguish of spirit and almost concludes that there is no mercy for him. In this case he may be told:

1. That there is no hope in any creature. He cannot help himself. He has no wisdom, power, nor worthiness that can help him. There is no way that he can take that which is sufficient for his deliverance; that ministers are not able to deliver him, and that, if others pray for him, yet that will not secure his salvation. All creatures are cyphers, and cannot work out any salvation for him. If God will destroy him, there is none that can save him.

2. That God may help him. It is not beyond the power of God to change his heart, and it is not beyond the grace of God to help him. The reason that men are not pardoned is not the greatness of their sins, but because they do not come to Jesus Christ. Though God is angry, he should not be discouraged. God is always angry with sinners when He comes to bestow converting grace upon them. God has done a great deal for him in as much as he makes him sensible of his danger. These discoveries of danger are many times forerunners of conversion. His condition is a great deal more hopeful now than when he pleased himself with his frames and attainments. Every man must despair in himself before he comes to trust in Christ. There is enough in Christ, *He is able to save to the uttermost,* Hebrews 7:15. Christ came to save the chief of sinners, 1 Timothy 5.

3. That there is no way left him now but to yield himself into the hands of God. If God destroys him, He may. He lies at the mere mercy of God. If God will deliver him, He may. If He does not He does no wrong. He cannot run from God, he cannot force God. If he stand it out against God, he takes a way to ruin himself. The safest course he can take is to fall into the hands of God. It may be that God may help him, however he can only perish.

SOMETIMES, a little before the work of God is completed in him, he complains that he seems to be as before he was under conviction, careless and senseless. His terrors have left him and he is not affected with his condition. In this case he may be told:

1. That now he may see what a heart he has, and how insufficient he is to deliver himself. His heart is empty of all that is good, and there is no possibility of his attaining salvation by his own power. He has no principle of grace and never had. The frames that he formerly had were nothing else but the workings of self-love and natural conscience and, unless God delivers him, he will never attain unto life.

2. That his way must be to wait upon God still. This is no sign that God has given him over. His terrors may quickly return again, and he may find mercy for all this. When he had his good frames and affections, they could not save him nor make his peace with God; and, if God shows him his own emptiness, he may quickly afterwards reveal to him the excellency of Christ.

At length, the man seems as if he were thoroughly brought off from himself and brought to lie at the foot of God. All his selfish hopes are taken away and he sees his own heart. His will bows, he seems to resign up himself to God. In this case:

1. It is best to examine whether there is no deceit in it. Sometimes it is so plain that there is no great occasion to examine; sometimes it is more doubtful. When they are thoroughly humbled, such things as these do concur.

(1) He sees his own righteousness to be utterly empty and vile, that it has no power to draw the heart of God. He sees nothing at all to commend him, but he has provoked God thereby.

(2) He is at an end of his contrivances to change his heart. Formerly, when things appeared dark unto him, he was wont to think that if he did thus or so, that would bring

him into a more hopeful way; but now he is beyond all his contrivances. He cannot do any more.

(3) He sees his heart spiritually dead. He is utterly destitute of power to do anything. Yes, he has no inclination to any good.

(4) He sees he is in God's hand. It is free for God to do as He will with him, and he resigns himself up to God, so he is more quiet now than he was, both because his will is brought down and he is satisfied that God can, and may, help him.

2. It is no way fit to tell a man that God will show mercy to him. For though this is the manner of God, when men are prepared for grace, to bestow grace upon them, yet there is no promise in the Scripture made to such persons. The promises are made to coming to Christ. Faith is the condition of salvation, and there are many promises made to humility. Yet there are none made to humiliation, and he is to be told that he is in God's hands. God is at liberty to do as He will with him, and that he must wait upon God to open his eyes and show Jesus Christ unto him.

3. It is very meet to set the gospel before him and mind him of God's sending Christ into the world to save sinners. Remind him that Jesus Christ has satisfied the justice of God and performed perfect obedience for us, that God has pardoned many sinners through Christ, that He offers salvation to him through Jesus Christ and that God has promised eternal life to all who accept Christ, that those who have nothing to bring with them shall be welcome to Him, that God is of infinite mercy and delights to glorify His grace in saving the chief of sinners, that because we had no worthiness God has provided a worthiness for us in Christ, that Christ is the author of eternal salvation to all that come to Him, that God's love is free and there is no danger in venturing upon Christ. *Whosoever believeth on Him shall not be confounded.*

QUESTION. Is there at that time any true meltings of heart because of sin? Is the soul truly grieved for its sins against God, as some men have thought?

ANSWER. Though there is such a conviction of sin as makes men to justify God, yet there is no godly sorrow for sin. Men are not at this time affected with any godly sorrow.

1. Because such sorrow is inconsistent with the work of humiliation. When the sinner is humbled, he sees himself emptied of himself and sees his own heart dead in sin. This could not be if he had any gracious sorrow for sin. If there were true sorrow for sin, there must be love to God, a spiritual understanding, a new heart, a divine principle put into the man, for nature cannot produce any such effect.

2. Because faith is the first act of grace. If the man had a gracious principle, he would immediately entertain Christ and the gospel. After a man has received a principle of regeneration, the first way that it works in is by drawing the heart to Christ. When men's hearts are changed and a new nature put into them, it does not first work in a way of sorrow for sin, or thirsting after God's glory, or delighting in holiness; but always the first act of grace is to close with Christ. God leads him into the exercise of this that he may be justified, Romans 5:1. If he did any other gracious act before this, it could not be accepted, for the person is not accepted before faith. All sanctification is the fruit of faith, Acts 26:18.

Soon after the soul is brought to lie at God's feet, he is wont to give an account of his closing with Christ; that God has revealed Christ to him and drawn his heart to him and he accepts Christ. In this case it is best:

1. To examine whether his faith is right. And in this work there is no weight to be laid upon it, whether it was in hearing, reading, praying, or meditating, that God gave the light to him. God does not confine Himself to any of those ways. Neither is there any weight to be laid on it, whether it

was by any particular word or without it. If it is according to the Word, it is sufficient. Nor must we lay weight upon it, whether it was by a word of promise or some other word in the gospel, nor whether he had one word come to him or many. Sometimes many promises flow in, one after another, in abundance, but special inquiry is to be made:

(1) What condition he was in just before, whether he was wholly emptied of himself or found any imaginary goodness in himself. If his humiliation was right, there is no doubt of his faith.

(2) Whether by that light that was given to him, he saw Christ and salvation offered to him, or whether he saw that God loved him or pardoned him, for the offer of grace and our acceptance goes before pardon and, therefore, much more before the knowledge of it.

(3) Whether he saw a glorious fullness in Christ, a sufficiency for the greatest sinners so as to make him admire the excellency of Christ.

(4) Whether the offer came with divine authority, whether he saw God calling him so that he could not but accept thereof.

2. If upon inquiry the case is more doubtful, as it may be, partly because some things were not so clear to himself, or because he has forgotten some material thing and cannot speak to it, it may be well to tell him that, if it is right, he will see more of it. When God begins to make a discovery of Christ, He will not leave men, but is wont to show them more. *The path of the just is like the morning light,* Proverbs 4:18.

3. If the case is plain, it is best to encourage him though there is no need to be positive. But he may be told that it is hopeful that God has drawn his heart to Christ and made a gracious change in his soul, and that if he does indeed believe on Christ, he shall certainly be saved. This sin does not make such a breach between God and him as to hazard his salvation.

4. To warn him to depend still on the free grace of God in Christ. He must expect many dark hours and times of temptation, but his way must be to grow in the knowledge of Christ. He must not think that now he shall always live a life of joy and comfort. Satan will be busy with him and he will have many workings both of carnal confidence and un-belief, and he must get more and more convinced of his own righteousness and the fullness of Christ. If he lives many years, he must never expect anything to glory in but Christ Jesus. And he is likewise to be warned that he lives up to the mercy of God in him, that he does not fall into a languishing and pining condition, but maintain the life and power of godliness so that he may not expose himself to temptation and darkness, and that he may not dishonor the holy name of God, showing forth the virtue of Him who has called him out of darkness into His marvelous light.

There are two particular cases that require a particular consideration. The first case is when a minister is sent for by a man upon his sick bed. The first thing to be done is to get an understanding in what condition the person is. For though a man who does not know his case may speak sev-eral things that may be safe and profitable, whatever his condition is, yet the more knowledge there is of the state of the man, the more advantage he is under to speak perti-nently.

1. If it is plain that the man is in a natural condition, it is most proper to insist upon these three things.

(1) That he has a present absolute necessity to be at peace with God, that if he should die in a natural condition, he will be forever undone. It is very fit that he should be reminded of his sinful life, and the dreadfulness of that pun-ishment that hangs over his head, which may be set before him in an affecting manner so that, if it is possible, he may be terrified and made sensible of those eternal miseries that are coming upon him.

(2) That he may not rest in anything short of Jesus Christ. Men in such a case are like a man drowning, ready to catch hold of anything that comes near. They are ready to have a dependence upon their privileges, upon their parentage, upon their sorrow for a misspent life, and upon their purposes to live better if God raises them up again. He must be led into an understanding of the strictness of the law of God and the vanity of all carnal confidences.

(3) That there is a glorious way of life prepared by Christ. Christ Jesus has fulfilled the law and wrought out eternal salvation for us. It must be insisted upon that the gift of God is eternal life, and that the mercy of God is free, and God does not refuse any who hearken to the call of the gospel; that God will as readily receive him if he comes to Christ as if he were likely to live many years and do service to God in the world.

And if his particular temptations may be discerned, care must be taken to remove them. If he is under any special discouragement or any flattering delusion, the snare, if it is possible, must be broken. He must be showed the vanity of that temptation. Such light must be held out that, if God will bless it, he may be delivered.

If, at that time or any other afterwards, he does not pretend to believe in Christ, it is very meet that he be cautioned that he does not deceive himself, for sickbed repentances are seldom true. Many persons who made great pretensions when sick have proved very bad after their recovery.

2. If it is doubtful whether the man is in a natural condition or converted, as there may be some occasion to hope because of his profession, because of his estimation among men, because of an orderly carriage, and yet occasion to fear; because there is no greater evil of grace, either in his conversation before or discourse at present. Sometimes there is more grounds for hope, sometimes for fear. These three things may safely be spoken to him.

(1) The doctrine of the law and gospel may be set before him. They may be somewhat explained and cleared up. It is fit that men should be reminded of the rule they are to be judged by. Many times when the rule is clearly laid down, conscience makes application, and witnesses to men how it is with them. Hebrews 4:12, *The Word of God is quick and powerful, sharper than any two edged sword.*

(2) Promises may be applied conditionally. He may be told that, if he has been thoroughly broken off from himself and brought to rely upon Christ, God has accepted him; that if his heart has been drawn by gospel encouragements to rely on Christ, he is out of danger; that if God's glory is upon his heart indeed, he is an heir of glory. He may be told that only his own conscience can tell what the workings of his heart have been; that if he is not mistaken, but has indeed made Christ his refuge, all his sins are pardoned.

(3) He may be warned so that he does not deceive himself. It may be meet to remind him that the heart is deceitful; that many false hearts go hoping out of the world; that there are several things that resemble faith, and every grace may be counterfeited; that he needs God to reveal things plainly to him; that it would be a dreadful thing to be mistaken. And so he may be charged that he does not trust in anything in himself, but trust himself to Christ alone.

3. If it is considerably plain that he is converted and gracious, either from his known eminency in religion or from an account that he gives of communion with God, or discoveries of Christ and gracious workings of his heart, it may be very meet to comfort him with those great and precious promises that God has made to remind him of the freeness of God's grace and the preciousness of the blood of Christ. He may be reminded of those things that are the pillars of our faith and the foundations of comfort; how God in all ages of the world has proposed this way of salvation, in this way the saints of old have lived and died; how the faithfulness of God stands engaged for their salva-

tion, that their sins and iniquities are cast behind God's back. This must be understood or spoken upon a supposition, that their work is a thorough work.

In case he desires the minister to tell him what he judges about his sincerity, it may be suitable to tell him that, as far as he can discern, his heart is upright, and that the root of the matter is found in him. He must tell him that he has no infallible knowledge. God alone knows the hearts of men. There is no depending on his judgment but, so far as he can perceive, his soul has been renewed by the Spirit of God.

If the man has any particular temptations, it is very suitable to remove them. He may be under temptation because he has great deadness, a great deal of pride and hypocrisy; because he has not had so much discovery of the favor of God as he perceives others have had; because God has afflicted him very much; because he is withdrawn now in the time of his sickness. Such particular temptations are to be answered. It may be showed to him that the dealings of God are various with His people; that such things are not inconsistent with grace; that the best way is to live upon the free mercy of God in Christ.

The other case is when such persons as have made a high profession of religion for a long while are in darkness about their condition. In this case, the first care of the minister must be to get satisfaction concerning the state of the person, whether he is regenerate or not. Not but that many things may be spoken that may be profitable to them, whether they are sincerely godly or not; but if the minister does not know their condition, he cannot apply proper remedies. And he may speak that which may be very dangerous if he supposes the man to be unconverted when he is converted. He may torment him and discourage him needlessly. If he supposes the man converted when he is not, he may do him much damage by comforting him up in a false way. Therefore, it is very needful that he gets what satisfaction he can about their condition so that he may be helpful to them in their distresses.

In order to his passing a right judgment upon their condition, he must be careful that he does not lay too much weight upon the fact that they have been in church fellowship many years, or that their carriage has been orderly, or that they are well accounted of where they live, for these are very fallible signs, such things as are common to saints and hypocrites. Though these things may be grounds of charity, a minister needs to have better grounds to go upon when he comforts up persons with hopes of reconciliation.

Neither must he lay too much weight on bad signs that are not demonstrative. If the man does not know the time of his conversion or first closing with Christ, if he has any notable blemish, if he is not well accounted of, the minister may not draw any peremptory conclusion from this that he is not godly. Yes, if he judges himself to be unconverted, it is best to inquire somewhat further in it.

It is best discovered by three sorts of inquiries.

1. Whether they have passed through the several steps of the work of conversion. Some can give so full an account thereof as will abundantly satisfy the minister that the work is right. Some are so strangely to seek that he may be much confirmed that they have no grace. In some others, after they have given what account they can, the work is more dubious.

2. Whether they have lived a life of sanctification. There is great diversity in the measures of sanctification that men have attained unto. Every holy man lives a holy life. The minister should inquire as to what knowledge they have of God. Do they prize the glory of God? Do they hate all sin? Do they draw their encouragement from Christ? Do they love holiness for holiness' sake? What conflict do they have with pride, unbelief, a self-righteous spirit, and self-love? A minister may come to competent satisfaction whether they are in a state of grace or not. In discoursing

such things with them, a man may, many times, feel the workings of a spirit of holiness.

3. Whether they have had sensible communion with God. God is wont at times to draw nigh to the souls of His people, sometimes in meditation, sometimes in prayer, and in other ordinances; and to make discoveries of Himself and of Jesus Christ to their souls, and to draw their hearts to him; and if there has been anything considerable that way, the minister may be well satisfied of their good estate.

In case the minister is satisfied that the man is not converted, he must use his prudence to judge whether it will be for the man's profit to tell him so in plain terms. Sometimes it may be a prejudice and a means to exasperate him. Sometimes there is no such danger, but he may freely tell him what he judges and the reasons of his judgment.

But in case he does not see it his way to tell the man his thoughts concerning him, yet he ought in conscience, in the wisest way he can, to put him in to the understanding of his own condition. He may not suffer the man to go away with an opinion that he thinks well of him, much less may he leave him ignorant of such rules whereby he may come to understand his condition. It becomes him to lay such signs of trial before him as are most likely to bring him to a sight of himself and convince him of his dangerous estate.

In case the minister is satisfied on good grounds about the man's good estate, he ought to endeavor to clear it up to the man, laying convincing light before him, and answering those temptations that make it doubtful to the man himself, and also to direct him in such ways wherein it is hopeful that God will help him and deliver him from his temptations.

APPENDIX

Three Sermons by the Reverend Mr. Stoddard

SERMON 1

The Spirit of the Lord is upon Me,
because He hath anointed me. Luke 4:18

This is a text Jesus Christ Himself preached upon at Nazareth, which was the place of His education. It is taken from Isaiah 61:1-2, where there is but little variation as to the words, but a great agreement as to the intention of them. The sermon that Christ preached is not upon record, but we have the preface, verse 21, *This day is the Scripture fulfilled in your ears,* which gives us some light and shows us that the prophecy relates unto Himself. In these words is a prediction of the Spirit's coming upon Him.

QUESTION. What is meant by the Spirit?

ANSWER. The third person in the Trinity.

God, Father, Son, and Holy Ghost are one and the same spiritual substance. But here the third person is understood. Sometimes He is called "the Spirit of the living God," 2 Corinthians 3:3; sometimes "the Spirit," 1 John 3:2, *I saw the Spirit descending from heaven;* sometimes "the Spirit of Christ," Philippians 1:19, *the supply of the Spirit of Christ;* sometimes "the Holy Spirit," Ephesians 4:30, *grieve not the Holy Spirit of God;* sometimes "the Spirit of Grace," Hebrews 10:29, *and have done despite to the Spirit of Grace.*

QUESTION. Why is the Spirit said to be upon Him?

ANSWER. It is all one as if the Spirit was said to be in

Him.

The same expression we have in 2 Kings 2:15, *The spirit of Elijah doth rest on Elisha,* and in Isaiah 11:2, *The Spirit of the Lord shall rest upon Him.* It may have a respect to the Spirit's visible descending on Him, Matthew 3:16, *He saw the Spirit of God descending like a dove, and lighting upon Him.*

This is amplified by the reason, *Because the Lord hath anointed Me.* The priests were separated to their office by this ceremony, Leviticus 8:12, *He poured of the anointing oil upon Aaron's head, and anointed him to sanctify him.* So the meaning is that God had separated and anointed Him to this office, to preach the gospel.

DOCTRINE. Ministers need to have the Spirit of the Lord upon them in order to the reviving of religion among His people. There are some times of degeneracy and declension in the church. Sometimes commonwealths are in a languishing way. Sometimes the estates of a people are under decay. So, sometimes, religion is in a withering condition; but there are means that are serviceable for the reviving of it, and this is one special means: when the ministers have the Spirit of the Lord upon them. The Spirit of the Lord must be poured out upon the people else religion will not revive. But when the Spirit is upon ministers, it is a very hopeful sign. Malachi 4:5-6, *I will send Elijah the prophet, and he shall turn the heart of the fathers to the children, and the heart of the children to their fathers, lest I come and smite the earth with a curse.* This was accomplished when God sent John the Baptist, who was filled with the Holy Ghost. So, after the apostles were filled with the Spirit, much was done by their ministry for the advancing of religion.

QUESTION. How is the Spirit's being upon ministers conducive to the reviving of religion?

ANSWER. Two ways especially.

1. The Spirit gives them a zeal for God's glory and the

salvation of souls. When the Spirit of God is upon them, they will be much concerned for God's glory. So it was with Elijah, 1 Kings 19:10, *I have been very jealous for the Lord God of Hosts.* They will not be indifferent whether God's kingdom flourishes or not. Their hearts will not be upon the world, but their hearts will be engaged for God's honor, and thus the salvation of men's souls. They will take a great deal of care that their hearers do not perish, 1 Corinthians 10:33, *Not seeking my own profit, but the profit of many that they may be saved.* 1 Corinthians 9:19-22, *I have made myself a servant of all, that I may gain the more, etc. I am made all things to all men, that by all means I may save some.*

(1) Hereby they are disposed to study and preach such things as do especially tend to the reviving of religion. There are several other truths that, in their season, must be studied and preached. Ministers must not decline to preach the whole counsel of God; no part of the Word of God is in vain. But when they are zealous for God's honor and men's salvation, they will set themselves to revive religion. They will dwell upon those things that more directly tend to the furtherance of men's salvation, such things as will take with the consciences of men. Ecclesiastes 12:10, *The preacher sought to find out acceptable words.* They will consider the necessities of people and strive to relieve them. So it was with Paul, Acts 20:21, *Testifying both to the Jews and also to the Greeks, repentance towards God and faith towards our Lord Jesus Christ.* The corruptions of the land will stir up their spirit, Acts 17:16, *While Paul waited for them at Athens, his spirit was stirred in him, when he saw the city wholly given to idolatry.*

(2) Hereby they are prepared to declare the Word of God powerfully. The Word of God is as a hammer, and men must smite with strength to make the nail enter or the rock to break. If the Word of God is preached in a dull, dead way, it is not likely to have much efficacy. Men will

be in danger to think that the preacher himself does not believe it, or that he lays no great weight upon it. But when they have a holy zeal, that makes them to be "Boanerges," sons of thunder, who will be earnest and fervent. That was the commendation of Apollos, that he was *fervent in spirit*, Acts 18:25. So did Christ teach, Matthew 7:29, *He taught as one having authority, and not as the scribes.* And this made His doctrine the more effective. Verse 28 says, *The people were astonished at His doctrine.*

This was foretold of Christ, Micah 5:4, *He shall tread and feed in the strength of the Lord His God.* Zeal will enflame the heart and make men declare the Word of God so as to awaken others and not lull them to sleep. Such men will speak in the heat of their spirits. When men are sensible of the breaking out of fire, or the approach of enemies, they will cry out earnestly. So the prophet directed in Isaiah 58:1, *Cry aloud, spare not, lift up thy voice like a trumpet, and show my people their transgression, and the house of Jacob their sins.*

(3) Hereby, they are filled with courage to dispense the Word of God faithfully. There is a danger that some men will be provoked if they are told plainly of their sins, if their confidences are shaken, and they are dealt with plainly. And if ministers do not have a spirit of zeal, they will be in danger of neglecting to speak what they should; and be apt to speak too tenderly. But if they have a spirit of zeal, that will make them faithful, Jeremiah 20:9, *His word was in my heart as a burning fire, shut up in my bones, I was weary with forbearing, and I could not stay.* They ought to speak whether men will hear or not. Ezekiel 2:7, *Thou shalt speak My words to them, whether they will hear, or whether they will forbear.* And zeal will make men faithful, though others are angry, Acts 2:36, *Let all the house of Israel know assuredly that God hath made this same Jesus whom ye crucified both Lord and Christ.* Zeal strengthens the heart against fear. So the prophet dealt plainly with Asa,

and John the Baptist with Herod.

2. If the Spirit is upon ministers, that gives them understanding and wisdom for their work. The Spirit of God makes them studious, busy in reading and meditating, and thereby they get understanding. The Spirit suggests suitable thoughts to them, and thereby they get understanding. The Spirit of God opens their eyes, gives spiritual discoveries to them, and thereby they get understanding. All wisdom comes from God. Men are led by the Spirit into the consideration of providences, and so they get a great deal of experience. God gave Solomon wisdom in a more than ordinary way, and He has His ways to give wisdom to men for the work to which He calls them. It was foretold concerning Christ that God would give wisdom to Him, Isaiah 11:2, *The Spirit of the Lord shall rest upon Him, the Spirit of wisdom and understanding, the Spirit of counsel and might, the Spirit of knowledge, and of the fear of the Lord shall make Him of quick understanding in the fear of the Lord.* God, by His Spirit, furnishes men with knowledge to be serviceable.

(1) Hereby He makes them able to reveal men's iniquities to them. Many men practice things that are evil under a notion of liberty. Through custom and carnal reason, and their dependence upon the judgment of others, they stand in the defense of sinful ways. They have a great deal to say in the vindication of them, and sometimes do not suspect them to be evil; but God, by giving understanding to ministers, enables them to lay convincing light before them and make it plain from the Word of God that those ways are evil. That is required of ministers, that they convince gainsayers, Titus 1:9. So Christ Jesus laid abundance of light before the Scribes and Pharisees to show them their iniquities. And Paul laid abundance of light before the Gentiles to show them their vanity and sin in worshipping idols. And Apollos laid light before the Jews to convince them of their sin in rejecting Christ, Acts 18:28, *He might-*

ily convinced the Jews, and that publicly, showing by the Scriptures that Jesus was Christ.

(2) Hereby they are made able to speak terror to the consciences of sinners. If the consciences of men are terrified, that makes way for their conversion. Terror of consciences makes way for men's coming to Christ, Galatians 3:24, *The law was our school-master to bring us to Christ.* And the Spirit of God, by giving them understanding, fits them for this work. Thereby they are enabled to represent in an affecting manner, the dreadful miseries that sinners are in danger of. So did John the Baptist, and the people of the publicans, and the soldiers were much affected and inquired what they must do, Luke 3:10,12,14. Ministers hereby are enabled to find out several considerations to evidence to men the certainty of their ruin if they continue in a natural condition, and to show the truth of that, Matthew 5:18, *Not one jot or tittle shall pass from the law, but all shall be fulfilled.* And they are able to convince men what danger there is that they will never be converted; to lay open the wretchedness of the heart and its mighty opposition to the gospel, the great advantages of Satan to seduce, the many by-paths that men are wont to take, the uncertainty of God's giving repentance to them, as the Apostle teaches in 2 Timothy 2:25, *If peradventure God will give repentance to the acknowledging of the truth.*

(3) Hereby they are able to reveal to men the deceits of their hearts. Man's heart is full of deceit, Jeremiah 17:9, *The heart is deceitful and desperately wicked, who can know it?* Men are wont to make plausible pretenses for their sins. They have many things to say by way of apology for themselves, excusing their sins. They pretend that they are willing to know their own hearts. They pretend that they see their own insufficiency. They pretend love to God and faith in Jesus Christ, but God, by His Spirit, enables ministers to lay open the deceitfulness of their hearts so that they are brought to know themselves. If men could hold their

deceits, they would live and die in hypocrisy, but God helps ministers to unravel their hearts, and so He leads them into an understanding of themselves, 2 Corinthians 10:4, *The weapons of our warfare are not carnal, but mighty through God, to the pulling down of strongholds.* Hebrews 4:12, *The word of God is quick and powerful, sharper than any two-edged sword, dividing asunder soul and spirit, joints and marrow, and is a discerner of the thoughts and intents of the heart.*

(4) Hereby they are made able to direct them in the right way. Men who are distressed in conscience are, many times, at an utter loss what to do, and are prone to run into by-paths and take very improper methods for their help. They are contriving in what way to get pardon and grace, and they would undo themselves; but God, by His Spirit, helps ministers to guide them in the right way, Malachi 2:7, *The priest's lips should keep knowledge, and they should seek the law at his mouth.* Ministers are to be their guide. It is their work to direct them so that they may not quench the motions of the Spirit; to direct them that they may not grow secure; that they may not settle on their own righteousness; that they may not get a false faith; that they may not be discouraged; that they may have no prejudices against God and His ways; that the work may be hastened, and that they may be led to Christ. Samuel tells the people that he will *teach them the good and right way,* 1 Samuel 12:23. So when God gives the Spirit to His ministers, they are fitted to lead sinners in the right way to Christ.

FIRST REASON. Men are so blind and corrupt that it is very difficult to work upon them. Men by nature are in darkness, Revelation 3:17, *Thou art blind.* They have wholly lost their spiritual sight, and their natural conscience is very defective. It is very slow to conceive of those things that it can conceive of. Men are subject to abundance of delusion. They are under prevailing of carnal reasonings, easily deceived with appearances and shows, subject to flatter themselves. They become *vain in their imaginations, and their foolish hearts are darkened,* Romans 1:21. And through heedlessness and forgetfulness, they are very ignorant of what they might know, Titus 1:15, *Their mind and conscience are defiled,* and the hearts of men are very much depraved. They are violently set on their carnal interests, Jeremiah 50:38, *They are mad on their idols.* They are exceedingly addicted to the love of the world. They are set for profit, pleasure, and honor. Their business is to advance their own interest. They cannot endure to reform their lives. They say as did Jeremiah, Jeremiah 2:25, *They have followed after idols, and after them they will go.* They are full of enmity to God and His ways, Romans 8:7, *The natural mind is enmity to God, is not subject to the law of God, neither indeed can be.* Hence, if they have but little means, ordinarily, they take very little impression.

Men who are fast asleep will not be awakened with a little noise. More gentle means will not do with naughty children. Small blows will not break a rock. Gentle medicine will not do for a stubborn disease. If ministers are ignorant and sluggish, there is little likelihood that much good will be wrought.

SECOND REASON. Yet men have so much conscience and self-love that it is difficult to withstand powerful means. Though sinful men are like the beasts that perish, yet they are not beasts. They have a conscience in them, and that tells them that there is a God who made heaven and earth; that He is to be served; that His anger is terrible and that His Word must be true. The Gentiles showed that *the work of the law was written in their hearts,* Romans 2:15. They have, likewise, a principle of self-love in them. They are craving happiness, Psalm 4:6, *who will show us any good?* They dread misery and abhor destruction. From these two principles, they are capable of being wrought upon. When the wrath of God is set before them in a lively manner, their consciences will echo to it. This rouses up sparks of light that are in conscience, and conscience adds its testimony. Hence the men are afraid. They tremble lest God should execute vengeance upon them. They would fain get their sins pardoned. When they hear the clear reasonings and powerful dispensations of the Word, they cannot but fear; and they think, "What shall I be profited if I should get the whole world, and lose my own soul?" So when they hear searching preaching, it leads conscience into the examination of their hearts and ways, and puts them upon it to labor after the power of godliness. A workman may bring rude timber into form. A skillful physician may be a means to remove a stubborn disease. Dull consciences may be frightened. Proper means may, by God's blessing, revive religion.

USE 1. The case of the Christian world is very sorrowful. A great part of the world makes a profession of Christ, but there is little sincere religion, very little of the power of godliness. And it may be said not of some particular persons only, but of some nations, as Revelation 3:1, *They have a name that they live, but they are dead*. There are great pretenses to religion, but God is but little honored, and few souls are saved. Religion does not flourish in many places, for the ministers do not have the Spirit of God upon them.

1. Some are heretical. There were an abundance of heresies in the days of the apostles, and there are many in these days. The Papists hold justification by works, that it is lawful to have images in worship; that the Pope is infallible and has the power to forgive sin, etc. The Socinians deny the doctrine of the blessed Trinity, the divinity of Christ, and that He bore the curse for us. The Arminians hold universal redemption, election from faith foreseen, the power of free will, and falling from grace. And they are ministers especially who propagate these opinions and beguile ignorant men. They pervert the Scripture and wrest it to their own destruction and the destruction of many others.

Learned men are the great seducers who promote damnable heresies. These men hinder the flourishing of religion. *They increase unto more ungodliness,* 2 Timothy 2:16. Men are *led captive by them,* 2 Timothy 3:6.

2. Some are wicked livers. They who should teach others to keep the law of God break it themselves. So it was with Hophni and Phineas, 1 Samuel 2:22, *They lay with the women that assembled at the door of the tabernacle of the congregation.* So it was afterwards, Isaiah 43:27, *Thy teachers have transgressed against Me.* So the Scribes and Pharisees, under the pretense of long prayers, did *devour widow's houses,* Matthew 23:14. And so it is at this day, in many places of the Christian world. Many who should lead men to heaven are guilty of debauched practices. They are swearers, drunkards, unclean, and profaners of the Sabbath. Religion is not likely to flourish under the influence of such men. Such teachers take a course to root religion out of the places where they dwell. They who teach wickedness by their practices are likely to do little good by their doctrine.

3. Some are ignorant. Many who are set up to teach have knowledge to read, and that is, in a manner, all the learning they have. Jereboam did not matter who he made to be priests. So it is with many others. God complained of old of the ignorance of teachers. Isaiah 56:10, *His watchmen are blind, they are all ignorant.* Men need a great deal of knowledge to be able to instruct others. But some teachers are ignorant of the principles of religion and are not able to vindicate them. They are not versed in the Scriptures. These men will be poor helps to the souls of others. Blindness is a very bad property in a guide. *If the blind lead the blind, both will fall into the ditch,* Matthew 15:14. When teachers are ignorant, *the people will be destroyed for lack of knowledge,* Hosea 4:6.

4. Some lack experience. Some ministers have good learning, a good conversation, and religious affections, and so they may do some good. They may be the means to

restrain some men from sin. Yes, they may be instruments of conversion; but such a ministry is not likely to revive religion in a land that does not have experiences. The condition of such a country is very sorrowful, Jeremiah 2:8, *They that handle the law know Me not.* It is a great blessing when people have such ministers as are able *to comfort others with that comfort wherewith they themselves have been comforted of God,* 2 Corinthians 1:4. Men who have had experience of temptation, and relief under them of their own hearts, and of Jesus Christ, are most likely to be instruments of the reviving of religion.

USE 2. Directing people what minister to choose. It is of great concern to have religion revived. God uses great means in order to do it. He brings great judgments and calamities in order to do it. But a special means to obtain this is to have such ministers as have the Spirit of God upon them. In Jereboam's time, they did not care who were priests, 2 Chronicles 13:9, *Whosoever cometh to consecrate himself with a young bullock, and seven rams, the same may be a priest of them that are no gods.* But if you desire the flourishing of religion, get such men for ministers that it may be said of them, as God said of Joshua, Numbers 27:18, *Take Joshua, the son of Nun, a man in whom is the Spirit, and lay thine hand upon him.*

But there is a double difficulty in this:

1. Some who are to choose do not regard this. In some places, the care of this matter belongs to the patron, and many times such have little regard to present those who are fit for the work. And where the people have a liberty to choose, they are careless in making a good choice. Some are purse-ridden, and do not care who they have, as long as they can have him upon easy terms. Micah got one on easy terms, and satisfied himself that he had a *Levite to be his priest,* Judges 17:13. Some love one who will prophesy smooth things, and nourish them in their vain hopes of eternal life, Isaiah 30:10, *They say to the seers, see not?*

And to the prophets, prophesy not right things, speak unto us smooth things, prophesy deceits. Some would have one who is a cheery companion. Some would have one who would please their itching ears, 2 Timothy 4:3, *After their own lusts they shall heap to themselves teachers having itching ears.* People who have but little religion are in danger of taking up with ministers who do not have the Spirit.

2. Some do not know where to find them. Some would be glad to get such a one, but they do not know where to suit themselves. We are not come to that pass that is spoken of in Amos 8:11-12, *I will send a famine in the land; not a famine of bread, nor a thirst of water, but of hearing the word of the Lord. And they shall wander from sea to sea, and from the north even to the east, they shall run to and fro to seek the word of the Lord, and shall not find it.* But yet there is not great plenty of such men as have the Spirit of God upon them. It is a mercy that people may find those that have good learning, and are orthodox in their principles, and of a good conversation; but there are not many who have the Spirit. People must take up with such as they can get. That which is lacking cannot be numbered.

THIRD USE. An exhortation to pray for ministers. It is the duty of ministers to pray for the people, and it is the duty of the people to pray for their ministers. The ministers are bound by their office to pray for the people, and the people are bound by their interest to pray for their ministers. When they pray for their ministers, they pray for themselves. Moses prays for them, Deuteronomy 33:8, *Of Levi he said, Let thy Thiummim and thy Urim be with thy holy One.* We find Paul several times begging the prayers of the church, Ephesians 6:18-19, *Praying with all manner of prayer and supplication, for all saints; and for me, that utterance may be given to me that I may open my mouth boldly, to make known the mystery of the gospel.* So 2 Thessalonians 3:1, *Finally, brethren, pray for us, that the word of the Lord may have free course, and be glorified even as it is with you.* Hebrews 13:18, *Pray for us.* This should move the people of God to pray for their ministers because, if the Spirit rests upon them, that is a preparation for the reviving of religion. It is a burden to the spirit of all godly men that there are such decays of religion; that few are converted and that iniquity so abounds and, therefore, you should be longing after that so that it may revive again.

Consider: 1. If religion does not revive, the country will become more wicked. Pride and wantonness, worldliness and profaneness abound in the land. There are many bad examples. There is a great deal of the breaking out of sin. In many places, they have a very ill name on the account of their iniquities. Many people declare their sin like Sodom and do not hide it. And how shall a stop be put to it unless religion is revived? Unless men are awakened and convinced? Ezekiel 36:25-27, *I will sprinkle clean water upon you and you shall be clean; from all your filthiness and from all your idols will I cleanse you. A new heart also will I give unto you, and a new spirit will I put within you, and I will take this stony heart out of your flesh and I will give you an heart of flesh. And I will put My Spirit within you, and cause you to walk in My statutes.* Some think family government may put a stop to sin. Some think the zeal of rulers, and faithfulness of officers, may put a stop to sin. But how shall these things be come at if the spirit of religion does not revive among us?

2. If religion does not revive, multitudes will perish forever. If religion does not revive, how shall men get to heaven? The form of godliness will not bring men to heaven. Coming to meetings, going to lectures, joining churches will not secure salvation. What will become of the posterity of the people of God if religion does not revive? Morality will not prepare men for dying, John 3:3, *Except a man be born again, he cannot see the kingdom of God.* If *men are converted, their sins will be forgiven,* Acts 3:19. But if they are not converted, they will not be forgiven.

Unregenerate men are very charitable to one another, but they will go to hell, Matthew 8:12, *The children of the kingdom shall go into outer darkness.*

3. If religion does not revive, there will be great judgments. We have had many sour calamities year after year; and there has been a great deal of consideration how to be delivered from the wrath of God. And something has been done for the preventing of wrath, but yet God's anger is not turned away. His hand is stretched out still. One judgment is scarcely over before another comes. We pray, we fast, we make laws, and dispute about reformation, but yet we are in affliction and the hand of God goes out against us. And so it will be unless there is a reviving of religion. Malachi 4: 5-6, *He shall turn the hearts of the fathers to the children, and the hearts of the children to their fathers, lest I come and smite the earth with a curse.* The curse of hardness of heart will not go alone. If God leaves us to a hard heart, that will be attended with other curses.

SERMON 2

To preach the gospel to the poor. Luke 4:18

In these and the following words is set forth the work that Christ was anointed for. First, to preach the gospel to the poor. Here mind:

1. What He was to preach; that is, the gospel. In Isaiah it is good tidings, and so the Greek word signifies, so our word "gospel" signifies. It comes from two Saxon words: God, that signifies good; and Spell, that signifies a word. There are other good tidings, but the gospel is so by way of eminency. The gospel brings tidings of the love of God to men, and of a glorious way of reconciliation and salvation. They are much to blame who slight the gospel and reject it. They carry on as if the gospel were not good tidings.

2. To whom He was to preach, viz., the poor.

There are two sorts of poor:

1. They that are low in the world; that are destitute of riches, and the invitations of the gospel are sent to them as well as others, and they who receive it are more generally of that sort. 1 Corinthians 1:28, *God hath chosen the base things of the world, and things that are despised.* James 2:5, *Hath not God chosen the poor of this world, rich in faith, heirs of the kingdom.* And Christ Jesus principally preached to such. Matthew 11:5, *The poor have the gospel preached unto them.*

2. Those that are poor in spirit, who are sensible that they have nothing to purchase heaven, who are sensible that they have no money nor price for their salvation. And they are of two sorts:

(1) Such as are legally poor, as those in Matthew 11:28, *That labor and are heavy laden,* who are convinced of the wretchedness of their hearts, and that God may justly

condemn them.

(2) Such as are evangelically poor in spirit, such as have the grace of humility, and live upon the mercy of God in Christ spoken of in Matthew 5:3, *Blessed are the poor in spirit, for theirs is the kingdom of heaven.* Those who are called poor here are called meek in Isaiah 60:1. Their hearts are meekened, either by conviction or by grace. I do not exclude the latter, but it seems to have a particular respect to the former.

DOCTRINE. The gospel is especially to be preached to the poor in spirit. They are particularly to be invited. Consider here these two propositions.

FIRST PROPOSITION. The gospel is to be preached to all. Though there is no expectation that all will receive it, yet it is to be preached to all. Ministers are not bound to preach it to everyone in the world, for that is impossible, but they are to preach to all as they have opportunity. They may not designedly hide the gospel from any. There are many differences among men, in respect of their estates, age, covenant, interest and sinfulness; but the gospel is to be preached to them all. Christ forbade His disciples to go into the way of the Gentiles, or to enter into any city of the Samaritans, Matthew 10:5, but this was a temporary command. But now, the gospel is to be preached unto all, Mark 16:15, *Go into all the world, and preach the gospel to every creature,* that is, every human creature. Acts 20:21, *Testifying both to the Jews, and also to the Greeks, repentance towards God, and faith towards our Lord Jesus Christ.* Galatians 3:28, *There is neither Jew nor Greek, there is neither bond nor free, there is neither male nor female, for ye are all one in Christ Jesus.* All are to be instructed in the gospel and to be invited to Christ.

The first reason is because the promise is to all. There is a conditional promise made to all who believe in Christ. There is no exception of any who believe in Christ. The sin against the Holy Ghost shall not be forgiven, but the conditional promise is true of them, and no man knows that he has committed that sin. The offer of the gospel is made to men without any exception. It is propounded in general terms so as to comprehend all. Acts 10:43, *Whosoever believeth on Him shall have remission of sins.* Men are ready to except themselves, but God makes no exceptions. Sometimes the promise is propounded indefinitely, John 3:36, *He that believeth on the Son hath everlasting life.* But sometimes it is propounded universally, for there is no other condition joined to this and, not only so, but the notes of universality are added to the promise, as "whosoever," John 3:16, and "all," Acts 13:39, or "any," Revelation 3:20. And, therefore, it must be preached to all.

The second reason is that they who are not poor in spirit may receive benefit by the gospel. The gospel is many ways useful to make men poor in spirit. Preparation for Christ is carried on by the law and the gospel in conjunction. When men hear that there is a way of salvation by Christ, that makes them more willing to see their danger, and not altogether so opposed to receiving conviction. It encourages them to pray to God to show them their misery. When men hear that Christ died for our sins, that makes them sensible that God is very angry for sin; that He will execute vengeance. This is an evidence of the justice and severity of God. Men may learn from thence that sin is a great offense and must be punished. Luke 23:31, *If they do such things in a green tree, what shall be done in a dry?* When men hear that *God so loved the world that He gave His only begotten Son* to suffer for them, this reveals the vile nature of sin whereby men abuse a God of such grace. Psalm 130:4, *There is forgiveness with Thee, that Thou mayest be feared.* When men hear that Christ has redeemed us from the curse, that may convince them that their own works cannot save them. Galatians 2:21, *If righteousness comes by the law, then Christ is dead in vain.* When they hear the command to believe in Christ, that convinces them that, though they are civil and religious, yet if they do not believe, they are rebellious and in a miserable estate.

The third reason is because they who are not poor in spirit now may be poor in spirit afterwards. If men hear the gospel and do not make right use of it now, yet they will retain the knowledge of it and it may do them service afterwards, though they are not sensible of their lost condition now, but are senseless and carnally confident, yet they may be poor in spirit hereafter. And then, what they have heard may come to mind and become powerful upon their hearts. It may be, when they do not have an opportunity to hear the gospel, they will call to mind what they have heard some years before, and ponder on what has been preached to them formerly. It is possible that they may be made poor in spirit when they are in captivity among the Papists or heathens. When they have no opportunity to hear the gospel, or they may be made poor in spirit when they lie upon a sick bed and cannot hear the Word preached, and then what they have formerly heard may work effectually on them. Manasseh would not hearken to the prophets when they spoke to him, 2 Chronicles 33:10, but afterwards, when he was a captive in Babylon, he remembered what he had been taught and repented. Verse 12 says, *When he was in affliction, he besought the Lord his God, and humbled himself greatly before the God of his fathers.*

SECOND PROPOSITION. The gospel is especially to be preached to the poor in spirit. It is fit that ministers should make a particular application of the calls of the gospel to them. It is true they may do so to young men, to ancient men, and to great sinners; but there is a peculiar reason to make particular application to them who are poor in spirit. These persons are, in a particular manner, invited in the Scripture, Isaiah 55:1, *Ho, every one that thirsteth, come ye to the waters, and he that hath no money; come ye, buy and eat, buy wine and milk without money, and without price.* They are thirsty who are parched up for want of something to quench their thirst. The like we have in Matthew 11:28, *Come unto Me, all ye that are weary and heavy laden, and ye shall find rest for your souls.* They are weary and heavy laden that are oppressed with the weight of God's wrath. So it is in Revelation 22:17, *The Spirit and the Bride say, Come. And let him that is athirst, come. And whosoever will, let him take of the water of life freely.* God is here teaching ministers to have particular regard to such. The invitations are not confined to these, but they are to be particularly applied to these. Some others have special need to have the terrors of the law preached to them; but the invitations of the gospel are especially to be propounded to those that are poor in spirit.

The reason for this is not from any excellency in this poverty of spirit. There is nothing of spiritual goodness in this. It is indeed a reasonable thing. It is according to the dictates of right reason, but there is nothing of piety or love to God, or godly sorrow in it. It is a mere forced thing and, accordingly, it is not acceptable unto God. The first good act that is done by the soul is believing in Christ and, accordingly, there is no promise made in the Scripture to this legal poverty of spirit. No man is under any promise of salvation until he comes to Christ. It is probable that God may give grace to all those who have this poverty of spirit; but there is no promise in the Word that he will. Indeed, there is an inconsistency in it that there should be any promise made to it. For when a man is poor in spirit, he owns that it is in God's liberty to do with him as he pleases; and he continues some time in this frame and continues to acknowledge it. But if there were any promise of salvation to it, then after the first act of submission, it would not be in God's liberty to do with him as He pleased. But he would be bound to bestow grace upon him, and he might challenge and lay claim to faith.

But the reason is because such men are prepared to receive the gospel. This poverty of spirit brings men near to

Christ, so that it is very hopeful that they will accept him.
The people of the Jews needed the ministry of John to prepare them to receive the Messiah, Mark 1:2, *I send my mes-
senger before thy face, to prepare thy way before thee.* So
particular souls need a work of preparation to make way for
their accepting of Christ. So Paul was prepared, Acts 9:6.
He, trembling and astonished, said, *Lord, what wilt thou
have me to do?* So said the jailer, Acts 16:30, *Sirs, what
must I do to be saved?* And when men are thrown out of
their own confidences, and made poor in spirit, they are
now in a fair way to receive Christ. Now they are sensible
that pardon and eternal life are the free gifts of God, and
therefore Christ, to prepare the angel of the church of
Laodicea, convinces him that he was *poor, and wretched,
and miserable, and blind, and naked,* Revelation 3:17. Yet
those men do not accept Christ until they have another
work of God upon the heart. They are not fully prepared by
this legal poverty of spirit. There needs to be another work
of God, further to prepare men before they will come to
Christ. If a man was poor in spirit seven years altogether,
that will not prevail with him to come to Christ; but further
to prepare him. His eyes must be opened to see the divine
authority of the gospel. 1 Thessalonians 2:13, *When ye received the word of God, which ye heard of us, ye received it
not as the word of men, but as it is indeed the word of God,
which effectually worketh in you that believe.* Until they see
the glory of God and Christ, they will not believe, Psalm
9:10, *They that know Thy name will put their trust in Thee.*
But when they are poor in spirit, they are prepared to receive the gospel and give entertainment to Christ.

    1. Now they see a lack of salvation. Men who are
seeking their felicity in the world, and do not have a sense
of the wrath of God, do not mind Christ. They take more
notice of the market and worldly opportunities than of
gospel invitations. Matthew 22:5, *They made light of it and
went one to his farm, and another to his merchandise.* But

when they are poor in spirit, they are like thirsty men who are even parched up. Revelation 22:17, *Let him that is athirst come.* They tremble as Paul did, Acts 9:6. This is some preparation.

2. Now they see that they can get salvation in no other way. If men have hope to work out their salvation themselves, they will not come to Christ. If they can cure their own souls, they will not come to this Physician. If the prodigal thinks that he can earn his living, he will not return to his father, Luke 15:15, *He went and joined himself to a citizen of the country.* But he who is poor in spirit has tried all conclusions, and everything fails him. He sees himself a dead man, Romans 7:9, *Sin revived, and I died.* So he sees greater necessity. This is a farther degree of preparation.

USE 1. Hence see that those who are not poor in spirit especially need to have the law preached to them. It is useful to all sorts of men to hear the preaching of the law. Saints stand in need of it to keep them humble, to put them upon it to renew their faith in Christ and to make them thankful; but especially such as are not poor in spirit. They need to be brought to Mount Sinai, and to hear the thunderings, and to see the lightnings. Secure sinners do not love to hear the terrors of the law. They would rather be entertained with some more comfortable doctrines; but they are in great necessity to hear the law. If there had been no law, there would have been no necessity of the gospel. And men who are not sensible of the terrors of the law will not regard the invitations of the gospel. Such as are not poor in spirit need to hear the law often so that they may be prepared to receive the gospel, that their hearts may be broken and humbled. Galatians 3:24, *The law was our schoolmaster to bring us to Christ.*

(1) That they may be sensible of the terribleness of damnation. Many men are not aware what a terrible thing it is to be damned. They have a deeper sense of poverty and reproach than they have a damnation. They look upon hell

as an uncomfortable place. They think if it must be their portion to go to hell, they shall bear it as well as others. They are not likely to go there alone. They seldom think of it. They look upon it as a remote thing, at a great distance, and it does not terrify them; but the law reveals that it is intolerable. Psalm 11:6, *Upon the wicked God will rain snares, fire and brimstone, and an horrible tempest.* Isaiah 30:33, *Tophet is prepared of old, he hath made it deep and large; the pile thereof is fire and much wood: the breath of the Lord, as a stream of brimstone, doth kindle it.* Matthew 25:41, *Depart ye cursed, into everlasting fire, prepared for the devil and his angels.* Matthew 13:42, *He shall cast them into a furnace of fire, there shall be weeping and gnashing of teeth.* Hence many men are exceedingly terrified and see a necessity of deliverance. Isaiah 33:14, *Sinners in Zion are afraid, trembling has surprised the hypocrites. Who among us can dwell with devouring fire? Who among us can dwell with everlasting burnings?* If the sense of the terribleness of damnation sinks into their hearts, they will not regard the world, they will not stick at their pains. They will not think much to part with their sins. They would rather undergo any sorrow than be damned.

(2) That they may be sensible of the great danger of damnation. Men are wont to soothe themselves that God will not send them to hell. He is kind and gracious, and they pray to Him. They are in covenant and enjoy privileges; they live orderly and are sorry for their sins, and so they hope they are in no great danger. But the law shows that sinners are under a sentence of condemnation. Romans 6:23, *The wages of sin is death.* The law shows that God is very angry with ungodly men, Psalm 50:21-22, *I will reprove thee, and set thy sins in order before thee. Consider this, ye that forget God, lest I tear you in pieces, and there be none to deliver.* The law shows that the threatening must be executed. The law must take place that the faithfulness of God is engaged for the fulfilling of the law. Matthew

5:18, *Not one jot or tittle shall pass from the law, but all shall be fulfilled.* Hence many men are afraid they shall not escape. They say as does Micah 6:7, *Will the Lord be pleased with thousands of rams, or ten thousands of rivers of oil?* They are afraid there is no mercy for them. They have a "fearful expectation of fiery indignation." They have a "dreadful sound in their ears," as we find in Job 15:21. And their hearts are meditating terror. They confess, they reform, they cry, they plead, but yet it rings in their ears, *Cursed is every one that continues not in all things that are written in the book of the law to do them.*

(3) That they may be sensible of the danger of sudden destruction. There is an inclination in men to put far away the evil day, and then they think they may have a long opportunity to enjoy worldly comforts. Men see that God exercises patience towards others, and they flatter themselves that He will be patient towards them. But by the law, they see that God will destroy many sinners suddenly. 1 Thessalonians 5:3, *When they say peace and safety, then sudden destruction cometh upon them, as travail upon a woman with child, and they shall not escape.* And the law shows them that God is very angry; that He sets their iniquities before Him, *their secret sins in the light of His countenance.* And so they are afraid God will not wait upon them. In the evening they are afraid they shall die before morning. If they find any bodily indisposition, they are afraid they shall die. If there is a thunderstorm, they are afraid they shall be killed. Their hearts shake at the report of sickness that prevails. They tremble at the shaking of a leaf. It is with them as in Deuteronomy 28:66-67, *Thy life shall hang in suspense, and thou shalt fear day and night, and shalt have none assurance of thy life. In the morning thou shalt say, Would God it were evening; and at evening thou shalt say, Would God it were morning; for the fear of thine heart wherewith thou shalt fear.*

(4) That they may be sensible of the justice of their

damnation. Men have an abundance of objections against the justice of God. They argue that sins do not hurt God; He is happy forever, notwithstanding their sins. They object that they could not prevent their sins, they are according to the decree of God; that they did not consent to sin, it was imputed to them, and so they were conceived in sin and born in iniquity. They object that they have done service and that the pains of hell are intolerable. But the law shows that their damnation is just, Romans 3:19, *Whatsoever things the law saith, it saith to them that are under the law: that every mouth may be stopped, and all the world may become guilty before God.* It is very evident from the law that men have deserved destruction; that they are worthy of death for they have broken a holy law and, according to the sentence of it, which is a rule of justice, they have merited damnation. It is evident that they are the proper causes of their own sins, and they have therein run upon the point of the sword, and have thrown themselves into a gulf of misery, Hosea 13:9, *O Israel, thou hast destroyed thyself.*

USE 2. Of warning to sinners. Do not be afraid to see that you are poor. There is he who makes himself rich, yet has nothing, Proverbs 13:7. So it is with some in this case, Revelation 3:17, *Thou sayest thou art rich, and increased in goods, and hast need of nothing, but art poor, and wretched, etc.* Men miserably deceive themselves by such imaginations, Galatians 6:3, *He that thinketh himself something when he is nothing deceiveth himself.* It is awful for men to see themselves poor. It is frightful but, if you are poor, it is best to see it. The case of such men is doleful, but not desperate. Such have no foundation to trust in themselves, but they have ground of encouragement, for the gospel is especially to be preached to them who are poor in spirit. In the invitations of the gospel, he has a singular regard to them, Luke 4:8. Your condition is not the more dangerous, but the more hopeful for seeing yourselves poor.

Consider:

1. You are wholly empty of goodness. Some of you have considerable shows of goodness. There is an appearance of good desires, gracious sorrow, love to ordinances and Sabbaths, and there is care to avoid sin; but there is nothing of goodness in all this. It cannot be said of you, as of Jereboam's son, *There is some good thing towards the Lord God of Israel.* All that you do is in hypocrisy. You are acted in your religion by a spirit of self-love. Fear of hell and hopes of heaven are the great principles that influence you. You are acted by a lust of self-love in all your religion, Psalm 78:36, *They flattered him and lied to him with their tongue. Their heart was not right with him.* You make a considerable profession, but God may say of you as of them in Deuteronomy 5:29, *O that there were such an heart in them.* All that you do is for yourselves, Hosea 10:1. If you are swept and garnished, yet you are empty. There is some similitude of faith and love, but no reality. There is not one spark of goodness in your heart. Though corruption is restrained, yet it reigns and, as long as corruption reigns, there is a total lack of goodness. Faith is the first good thing that is wrought in the heart. You are afraid of judgment; so are the devils, James 2:19, *The devils believe and tremble.* You are much in prayer; so would the devils be if the had hopes of deliverance.

2. You have no power to do any good. You have power to do all manner of external duties, but you have no power to keep the law. Romans 8:7, *The natural mind is not subject to the law of God, neither indeed can be.* If you have the help of ordinances, of afflictions, of deliverances, of examples, yet you cannot work up any gracious frame in your own heart. If there were a seed of grace in your heart, by being cherished it might grown and flourish, but there is none. A man who is in a swoon may be brought to be sensible, and to walk and work, but a man that is dead cannot. Thus it is with you. You are *dead in trespasses and sins,*

Ephesians 2:1. A watch or a clock, by springs and weights, may move briskly, but it has no principle of life. It is quite beyond you to do any spiritual good. You cannot receive the gospel. There is encouragement enough set before you, and it would be exceedingly profitable to you to receive it, but you cannot. You do not have a heart to receive it, John 6:44, *No man can come unto Me, except the Father that sent Me draw him.*

 3. God is not bound to change your heart. God is absolutely free. He may help you but, if He will not, He is blessed forever. It is true, He may help you without any wrong to Himself, but that lays Him under no necessity. It is His choice whether He will glorify His justice or His mercy on you. He may pass over you and take another. Romans 9:16, *It is not of him that willeth, nor of him that runneth, but of God that showeth mercy.* God is under no constraint to change your heart. His justice does not necessitate Him. You have deserved condemnation, and your prayers and tears lay no bonds on the justice of God. His faithfulness does not necessitate Him. He has promised to convert some, but there is no absolute promise to any natural man. His mercy does not necessitate Him. The merciful nature of man, many times, forces him to pity and help others, but God is wholly voluntary in the exercises of His mercy. God is not of such a tender heart that he cannot bear to see men in misery. God can take pleasure in the exercises of justice. Isaiah 1:24, *Ah, I will ease Me of mine enemies, and avenge Me of My adversaries.* His honor does not necessitate Him to convert you. It would have been as much for His honor to have converted Esau as Jacob, Judas as Peter, Saul as David. If he does not convert you, He will be glorified forever. You cannot bring God under any necessity to convert you. If He does not, He does you no wrong; you are in His hands. He is the potter and you are the clay. He may make you a vessel of honor or dishonor, Romans 9:21.

USE 3. Of exhortation to them that are poor to receive the gospel. If it were not offered to you, it would be obtrusion and presumption, a thrusting of yourselves upon Christ; it would be an impudent thing. But God offers mercy to you; yes, in a special manner, as the message concerning Christ's resurrection was sent in a particular manner to Peter. So He charges His ministers to make a particular application of the gospel to you, Luke 4:18, Isaiah 55:1, Revelation 22:17. Consider:

1. It is not beyond His mercy to pardon you. Salvation is a great work. If your sins had been fewer in number, and smaller in their nature and aggravations, it would require great mercy to pardon and save you. But as great as your sins are, it is not beyond the grace of God. You must beware that you *do not limit the holy One of Israel.* Ephesians 2:4, *God is rich in mercy.* His grace is like the ocean, it is sufficient to cover all your sins. Ephesians 3:18, *to comprehend the breadth, and length, and height, and depth of the love of Christ.* There are three dimensions that belong to bodies; here are four ascribed to mercy. Thickness may be measured downwards, so it is depth; and upwards, so it is height. Mercy brings sinners from deep misery to the pinnacle of happiness. God's mercy is greater than man's. God can find mercy for such as men cannot find mercy for. Hosea 11:9, *I will not return to destroy Ephraim, for I am God and not man.* Isaiah 55:9, *For as the heaven are higher than the earth, so are My ways higher than your ways, and my thoughts than your thoughts.* God's mercies are greater than your sins. Men think if they had not sinned so much, or so long, their sin would not have been beyond God's mercy. But God's mercy can conquer all their provocations. Grace may prevail over all, Romans 5:21, *Grace reigns through righteousness unto eternal life.*

The mercy of God is greater than we can conceive of. The understanding of man is large. We can conceive of how many minutes there are in a thousand years; how many

inches there are to the center of the earth, but we cannot
comprehend the love of Christ. Ephesians 3:19, *the love of
Christ passeth knowledge.* We cannot comprehend the bitterness of the cup that He drank for our sakes. We cannot
comprehend the duration of His love. We cannot comprehend the great good that He has procured for us.

2. God has designed to save many lost sinners. It is the
purpose of His heart to bring many poor sinners to heav-
enly glory. If He had taken up a resolution against it, men
might well be discouraged; but He has not resolved against
it, neither is He at a loss what to do. His not loath to do it;
but it is His full determination. He is resolved in His way,
and He purposes to break over all objections and conquer
all oppositions. He is set in His way and will not be put out
of it. 2 Thessalonians 2:13, *God has chosen you to salvation.* Galatians 1:5, *Having predestinated us unto the adoption of children by Jesus Christ.* And He has done a great
deal in order to the salvation of such sinners. The price of it
is paid. Sin laid a bar in the way, but that bar is removed by
the death of Christ. There is no need of any contrivance
how to satisfy the law, that is done already by Christ. God
has sent Christ to save us. Galatians 3:13, *Christ redeemed
us from the curse, being made a curse for us.* And God
makes a proposal to you, and gives you liberty to be saved,
if you will accept Jesus Christ. He does not tell you that His
heart is hardened against you; but He tells you that you
shall be welcome if you will come to Christ. Revelation
22:17, *Whosoever will, let him take the water of life freely.*
Yes, He beseeches you to come for salvation. God is of infinite majesty, yet He entreats you to be saved. He conde-
scends to your infirmity and stoops so low as to plead with
you. He becomes, as it were, a petitioner to you. He begs
you to come, and urges it as a courtesy to come, with ten-
der-heartedness He prays you to come. 2 Corinthians 5:20,
*We are ambassadors for Christ, as though God did beseech
you by us; we pray you in Christ's stead, be ye reconciled*

to God.

3. This is a principal way wherein God glorifies Himself. The end of all things is God's glory, and He has done many great things for His glory. He made the world for His glory that His power and wisdom might be manifested. He preserved the holy angels from sinning for the glory of His goodness. He gave the law for the glory of His holiness. He drowned the old world, saved Israel out of Egypt, destroyed Sodom, brought Judah from Babylon for His glory. But this is a principal way wherein He glorifies Himself in working out the salvation of sinners by Christ. There is a great manifestation of the Trinity of Persons in the God-head. There is a manifestation of the power, of the justice, and of the manifold wisdom of God and of His unsearchable grace. In this way, He is greatly exalted. Micah 7:18, *Who is a God like unto thee, pardoning iniquity, and passing by the transgression of the remnant of His heritage because He delighted in mercy.* Revelation 5:12-13, *Worthy is the Lamb that was slain, to receive power, and riches, and wisdom, and honor, and strength, and glory, and blessing. And every creature which is in heaven, and in the earth, and under the earth, and such as are in the sea, and all that are in them, heard I, saying, Blessing, and honor, and glory, and power be unto Him that sitteth on the throne, and to the Lamb forever and ever.*

PREFACE TO SERMON 3

Those who have been eminent reformers in the Church of God have seldom or never been so happy as to effect a perfect reformation. Asa reformed many things, but the high places were not taken away, 2 Chronicles 15:17. And though it is said of Jehoshaphat that *he took away the high places out of Judah*, 2 Chronicles 17:6, yet, chapter 20:33, it is noted that in the latter end of his reign that the high places were not taken away. The meaning is that he took them away in part, yet did not perfectly effect it. Corruption is wont to creep upon the church by degrees, and reformation is not effected at once. Sometimes, when those things that are more gross are taken away, some lesser corruptions are retained and, sometimes, when men go from one extreme, they don't stop where they should, but trespass on the other hand. This comes to pass partly though the dim-sightedness of men. When many corruptions are grown up in the Church, it must be a work of time to make a discovery of them. Those who discern some are not suspicious of others. When the Church is much corrupted it is a time of darkness, and errors do not lie open to observation. Partly, it comes to pass through the perverseness and stubbornness of people who are backward to turn out of those ways that they have been naturalized unto; that is given as the reason why the high places were not taken away *because the people had not prepared their heart to the Lord God of their fathers,* 2 Chronicles 20:32.

There have been three remarkable instances in these later ages of the imperfect accomplishment of the work of reformation. Luther was an instrument in the hand of God to open a door of deliverance from popery, and he, with an abundance of evidence, made a discovery of a multitude of abominations in the church of Rome, yet was so unhappy as to fall into that corrupt opinion of consubstantiation.

The glorious reformers of our nation in the days of King Edward the Sixth went beyond Luther in the work of reformation and, yet, even that glorious reformation was very imperfect and lacking in many things to be mended by the church in succeeding ages. And those holy men who first planted this land carried on the work of reformation to a higher pitch, yet failed in several things; especially in two points, viz., in not accepting non-scandalous persons into their communion, and in not acknowledging public government in the church.

And such is the misery of the Church of God that the mistakes of those worthy men who have led in the work of reformation prove an invincible temptation to many men. As the renown of those reformers is a bulwark against those errors that were exploded by them, so we find ourselves embarrassed by their mistakes from proceeding in the work of reformation, as if it were criminal not to mistake with them.

It may possibly be a fault and an aggravation of a fault to depart from the ways of our fathers; but it may also be a virtue and an eminent act of obedience to depart from them in some things. Men are wont to make a great noise that we are bringing in innovations and departing from the Old Way. But it is beyond me to find out wherein the iniquity lies. We may see cause to alter some practices of our fathers without despising them, without priding ourselves in our own wisdom without apostasy, without abusing the advantages that God has given us, without a spirit of compliance with corrupt men, without inclinations to superstition, without making disturbance in the church of God. And there is no reason that it should be turned as a reproach upon us.

Surely it is commendable for us to examine the practices of our fathers. We have no sufficient reason to take practices upon trust from them. Let them have as high a character as belongs to them, yet we may not look upon

their principles as Oracles. Nathan himself missed it in his
conjecture about building the house of God. He who believes principle, because they affirm them, makes idols of
them, and it would be no humility, but baseness of spirit for
us to judge ourselves incapable to examine the principles
that have been handed down to us. If we are any way fit to
open the mysteries of the gospel, we are capable to judge
these matters. And it would ill become us so to indulge ourselves in ease as to neglect the examination of received
principles. If the practices of our fathers in any particulars
were mistakes, it is fit they should be rejected. If they are
not, they will bear examination. If we are forbidden to examine their practices, that will cut off all hopes of reformation.

The design of the following discourse is to examine one
practice of these churches which is thought to be a failing.
It was not composed on a design to be made public, but the
importunity of some gentlemen who heard it has prevailed
for the printing of it.

All that I request of the reader is that he does not act
like those who told the prophet, Jeremiah 44:16, *As for the
word which thou hast spoken to us in the name of the Lord,
we will not hearken to thee.*

SERMON 3

The Inexcusableness of Neglecting the Worship of God Under a Pretense of Being in an Unconverted Condition

All the congregation of Israel shall keep it. And when a stranger shall sojourn with thee, and will keep the Passover to the Lord, let all his males be circumcised, and then let him come near and keep it: and he shall be as one that is born in the land: for no uncircumcised person shall eat thereof. (Exodus 12:47-48)

In this chapter, we have the institution of the Passover, and the several laws and ordinances, that were to be attended in the celebration of it, 2 of which are set down in these verses. First, verse 47, *All the congregation of Israel shall keep it.* This must be understood with its exceptions. Those who were unclean were not to keep it until they were cleansed. Numbers 9:13, *The man that is clean and is not in a journey, and forbeareth to keep the Passover, even the same soul shall be cut off from his people.*

Another exception was the females. Women were not bound to go to the place which God should choose where the Passover was to be kept. Exodus 23:17, *Three times in the year shall all thy males appear before the Lord God.* Yet, when they were present they were bound to keep it. Exodus 12:4, *If the household be too little for the lamb, let him and his neighbor next unto his house, take it according to the number of the souls.* Most probably also, they who were cut off from their people by a sentence of excommunication, were not to keep it.

Secondly, verse 48, the stranger is allowed to keep it upon two conditions: (1) That he desired it. Sometimes

strangers who dwelt among them became proselytes and
desired to keep this ordinance. As they were not to be com-
pelled, so they were not to be rejected, if they desired it in
an orderly way. (2) That all his males were circumcised.
Circumcision was a token of God's covenant. When they
were circumcised, they were incorporated and became as
those who were born in the land, and enjoyed equal privileges with natural Israelites.

The doctrine to be spoken to is that sanctifying grace is
not necessary unto the lawful attending of any duty of worship. The whole congregation, whether sincerely godly or
not, was to keep to the Passover. Sanctifying grace is an
inestimable blessing, far beyond all the common gifts of the
Spirit. It is the very life of the soul, it fits it to serve God
and to enjoy communion with Him. Sanctifying grace is
necessary to salvation; without holiness no man can see the
face of God. Yes, sanctifying grace is necessary to the acceptable attendance of every duty of worship. If men were
not holy, their offerings were not acceptable, nor their sacrifices sweet to God; but sanctifying grace is not necessary
to the lawful attending of any duty of worship. If men are
not holy, yet it is lawful for them to attend any duty of worship. No duty of worship is forbidden to men because they
are destitute of sanctifying grace. From the beginning of the
world to this day, men were never forbidden any duty of
worship for lack of sanctifying grace.

Sanctifying grace is necessary unto the right discharge
of moral duties as well as instituted; but it is not necessary
unto the lawful attending of moral duties, or the lawful attending of instituted duties; and as men may not excuse
themselves from moral duties for the lack of grace, so they
many not excuse themselves from any duty of worship.

I shall clear up the truth of this doctrine by an induction
of particulars.

1. Sanctifying grace is not necessary unto the attending

of those duties of worship which are required in all ages. There are some duties of worship that are not peculiar either to the state of the church in the time of the Old Testament or of the New, but common to both. And they may be attended by such as are godly and such as are not. Men in a natural condition may lawfully attend them. Men's being in a natural condition is no sufficient pretense for neglecting them, as:

(1) Prayer. Such men's prayers are an abomination unto God, Proverbs 28:9, *He that turneth away his ear from hearing the law, even his prayer shall be abomination.* Yet they are to be performed. It is the duty of all men to pray to God, Luke 18:1, *He spoke a parable to them to this end that men ought always to pray.* The Pharisees were blamed by Christ for praying in the streets that they might have glory from men, and for making long prayers for a pretense, but they are not blamed for praying. Ungodly men are much blamed in Scripture for not praying, Psalm 14:4, *They call not upon God;* Isaiah 43:22, *Thou hast not called upon Me, O Jacob.* So men are blamed for leaving off praying, Job 27:10, *Will he always call upon God;* and chapter 36:13, *they cry not when he bindeth them.* All sorts of men are directed to cry to God in their necessities. Sinners are put upon it to cry to God, Isaiah 55:6, *Seek ye the Lord while He may be found, call ye upon Him while He is near.* Such as are ungodly are stirred up to pray to God for forgiveness, Acts 8:22, *Pray God if perhaps the thought of thy heart may be forgiven.* It was the manner of the people of Israel good and bad to pray, Luke 1:10, *The whole multitude of the people were praying without at the time of incense.*

(2) Hearing the Word. Men must assemble themselves on the Sabbath to hear the Word, Leviticus 23:3, *The seventh day is a Sabbath of rest and holy vocation.* Ungodly men must do it in order to their conversion. The Word of God is the means of conversion, James 1:18, *Of*

His own will begat He us by the word of truth. The Word of God teaches men to turn to God; it holds forth conviction, warning, encouragement and direction. Romans 10:14, *How shall they believe on Him of whom they have not heard?* The Word of God is the means of regeneration, Psalm 19:7, *The law of the Lord is perfect, converting the soul.* Therefore, ministers must preach the Word to all sorts of men, good and bad. Christ preached to the multitudes, Matthew 5:1-2. So did John the Baptist, and so did the Apostles. And it is spoken of as a very bad thing for men to withdraw themselves from the assemblies of the people of God, Hebrews 10:25. Yes, it is lawful to preach the Word of God to the heathen. There was a temporary command to the disciples that they should *not go into the way of the Gentiles,* Matthew 10:5, but afterward they were commanded to teach all nations, Matthew 28:19. They were told to go into all the world and preach the gospel to every creature; and, if it is lawful to preach to them, it is lawful for them to hear it.

(3) Preaching the Word. It is upon all accounts most desirable that preachers should be godly men and *caeteris parisbus.* They who are converted themselves are most likely to be instruments of the conversion of sinners, and the edification of saints. Yet it is lawful for men in a natural condition to preach the Word. Christ Jesus sent out Judas to preach the gospel as well as the other disciples, Matthew 10:7. It was the work of the Priests and Levites to preach to the people of Israel, Deuteronomy 33:10, *They shall teach Jacob thy judgments, and Israel thy law.* But we have no reason to think that they were all godly. God gave extraordinary gifts in the primitive times to some who were not godly, to fit them for preachers, 1 Corinthians 13:1, *If I speak with the tongue of men and angels, and have not charity,* etc. Christ directed the people to attend on the preaching of the Scribes and Pharisees. *The Scribes and Pharisees set in Moses seat; whatsoever therefore they bid*

you observe, that observe and do. And Paul rejoiced in some men's preaching of Christ, though they did it with a bad spirit, Philippians 1:18.

2. Sanctifying grace was not necessary unto those duties of worship that were peculiar to the times of the Old Testament. There were several acts of worship that were instituted of old, but have been abolished long since. When they were divine institutions, they were to be attended not only by godly men, but also by natural men. As:

(1) Circumcision. Circumcision was a holy ordinance, a token of the covenant between God and His people; but multitudes of people were, according to the ordinance of God, to be circumcised in the flesh who were not circumcised in heart. God never blamed the people of Israel for circumcising persons who were not regenerate. Abraham was appointed to circumcise all the males in his family, Genesis 17:12-13. Ishmael was circumcised, but yet a carnal person, Genesis 17:25. When the Israelites bought servants from among the heathen, they were bound to circumcise them. All the Israelitish male children were in their several generations to be circumcised, yet there were but a few of them that proved godly. God ordered that the congregation of Israel should be circumcised at Gilgal, Joshua 5:2, *At that time the Lord said unto Joshua, Make thee sharp knives, and circumcise again the children of Israel the second time;* yet multitudes of them were carnal men.

(2) The Passover. This was a memorial of the angels passing over the houses of the Israelites, when the first born of the Egyptians were slain, Exodus 12:27, which was a type of our redemption by Christ. Therefore, Christ is called our Passover, 1 Corinthians 5:7, *Christ our Passover is sacrificed for us.* And it was lawful for men to partake of the Passover who were not regenerated, for it was God's appointment that the whole congregation should keep it, Exodus 12:47. At the time of the first institution, there were very few godly among them, for they are called "an evil

generation." And so they are called many other times, yet God threatens those who, under any pretense, neglected to celebrate the Passover if they were clean and not on a journey, Numbers 9:13. And Hezekiah sent to invite the people of Ephraim and Manasseh, and other tribes, to celebrate the Passover, though they had lived in idolatry for some ages, 2 Chronicles 30:1, *And Hezekiah sent to all Israel and Judah, and wrote letters also to Ephraim and Manasseh, that they should come to the house of the Lord at Jerusalem to keep the Passover to the Lord God of Israel.* And Jesus Christ Himself partook of the Passover along with Judas, Luke 22:13-14, *They made ready the Passover, and when the hour was come, He sat down and the twelve Apostles with Him.*

(3) Offering sacrifices. Many times the whole congregation of Israel offered sacrifices to the Lord, 1 Chronicles 29:20-21, though multitudes of them were in a natural condition. Any one of the people of Israel had his liberty, as he saw occasion, to bring his sacrifice to the Lord, Leviticus 1:2. Yes, not only the people of Israel, but the strangers among them had liberty to bring their sacrifices, Leviticus 22:18-19, *Whoever he be of the house of Israel, or of the strangers in Israel that will offer his oblation for all his vows, and for all his freewill offerings, which they will offer unto the Lord, for a burnt offering; Ye shall offer it at your own will, a male without blemish.* And in many cases the people of Israel were bound to bring their offerings, so the sin offerings for sins of ignorance, Leviticus 4. Thus it was with the trespass offerings for sins wittingly committed, Leviticus 6:10. So when they were cleansed from leprosy, and also in many other cases, they indeed did it in a very provoking way because they lived in wickedness, Jeremiah 6:20. He tells them *their offerings were not acceptable, nor their sacrifices sweet to him.* But it was lawful for them, whether regenerate of unregenerate, to bring their sacrifices.

(4) Officiating in the work of the priesthood. The priests, besides teaching the people, were bound to many other services: the offering of sacrifices at the brazen altar, the setting of the shewbread in order, the lighting of the lamps, the offering of incense, the judging in cases of leprosy, and in all ecclesiastical cases. But if they were not regenerate, yet it was lawful for them to officiate. If they had any blemish they might not, Leviticus 21:17, but the lack of regenerating grace did not make it unlawful for them to officiate. The priesthood went by lineal descent from Aaron. It belonged to them by generation, not by regeneration; and it is unreasonable to think that all the posterity of Aaron were regenerate. Hophni and Phineas were not, 1 Samuel 2:12, *The sons of Eli were sons of Belial, they knew not the Lord.* And the chief priests were principal enemies to Jesus Christ.

3. Sanctifying grace is not necessary unto the attending such duties of worship as are peculiar to the times of the New Testament. There are a few duties of worship that are peculiar to these times of the New Testament, but there's no peculiar qualifications requisite in those who attend them. They agree with the worship in the time of the Old Testament, so that they are to be attended by members of the visible church. As:

(1) Baptism. In adult persons, it is needful that there be profession of faith and repentance, morally sincere, in order to their being baptized, Matthew 3:6, *They were baptized of John in Jordan, confessing their sins.* So the Eunuch, before his baptism, made confession of Christ, Acts 8:37, *I believe that Jesus Christ is the Son of God.* But baptism may be administered to those who are not regenerate. It is not to be imagined that all who were baptized by John were regenerate, or judged by him to be so. If regeneration had been necessary unto baptism, Christ would not have committed that work to His disciples, who were then exceedingly raw, John 4:1-2, The Pharisees *heard that*

Jesus made and baptized more disciples than John, though Jesus Himself baptized not, but His disciples. So there were multitudes baptized by Philip in Samaria, and Simon Magus among the rest, Acts 8:12-13. And it is the appointment of God that the children of His visible people should be baptized, who are generally at that time in a natural condition. If unregenerate persons might not be baptized, the Pharisees would not have been blamed for neglecting baptism. They would have been excused as not being prepared for it; but they are condemned for not being baptized, Luke 7:30, *The Pharisees and Lawyers rejected the counsel of God against themselves, not being baptized of Him.*

(2) The Lord's Supper. No scandalous person may be admitted to baptism, neither may any scandalous person be admitted to the Lord's Supper; but those who are not scandalous may partake of it, though they are not regenerate. Such persons as might lawfully come to the Passover may also, if they have knowledge to discern the Lord's body lawfully, come to the Lord's Supper, for they are alike figures. The Passover was a type of Christ to die; the Lord's Supper is a representation of Christ who has died. It is lawful for unregenerate men to celebrate the memory of the death of Christ, which is a great encouragement and comfort unto them, and so they do in this ordinance. It is lawful for unregenerate men to give a solemn testimony to the virtue of the death of Christ and show it forth, and so they do in this ordinance, 1 Corinthians 11:26, *Ye show forth the Lord's death till He come.* That which God teaches us in this ordinance is very needful for unregenerate men to learn, namely, the insufficiency of all other things besides the death of Christ for salvation, and the all-sufficiency of Christ for salvation. That which we profess in this ordinance is very fit for unregenerate men to profess; namely, the need of Christ and saving virtue of His blood. As it may be of great advantage to natural men to hear God's promise in the Covenant of Grace, so to see God

setting His seal to the Covenant of Grace. If it is lawful for all the adult members of the church to partake of the Lord's Supper, then it is lawful for some unregenerate men to do it; but it is lawful for the all the adult members of the church to do it. This was the practice in the primitive church, 1 Corinthians 10: 17, *We are all partakers of that one bread.*

If it is lawful for the church to require unregenerate persons to come to the Lord's Supper, then it is lawful for them to come; but it is lawful for the church to require all its adult members to keep the covenant with God. If it is lawful for an unregenerate man to be in covenant with God, it is lawful for them to come to the Lord's Supper for, if it is lawful for them to be in covenant, it is lawful for them to keep covenant.

If sanctification were a necessary qualification to partaking in the Lord's Supper, then it would be a very sinful thing for any unsanctified person to come, though he hoped he was godly, though he was confident of his godliness. When Christ instituted this ordinance, He commanded His disciples to attend it, Luke 22:19. Therefore, it is an ordinance to be attended by the whole church, by all the disciples of Christ who have knowledge. If sanctification were a necessary qualification, in order to partaking, then the church should let no others come, and then God would have given them a certain rule in attending of which they might keep all others away. Men need to have good arguments to make the world believe that coming to the Lord's Table is a privilege equally confined with justification, adoption, and eternal glory, and that none may venture to the Lord's Table but those who shall be admitted into the Kingdom of Heaven.

(3) Officiating in the work of the gospel ministry. If a man knows himself to be unregenerate, yet it is lawful for him to administer baptism and the Lord's Supper. The blessing of this ordinance does not depend upon the piety

of him who administers it. Christ knew Judas to be unregenerate, yet He let him, as well as the rest of the disciples, administer baptism, John 4:2, *Jesus baptized not, but His disciples*. If men are destitute of regenerating grace, yet they may administer God's ordinances in such a manner as may be for the glory of God and the edification of His people. It is most desirable upon all accounts that they who officiate in the work of the ministry be holy and gracious men; but men who are destitute of grace are not prohibited in the Word of God to administer the ordinances of God. If such may preach, surely they may administer sacraments. Paul speaks of preaching as a greater work than administering baptism, 1 Corinthians 1:17, and we may argue that it is greater than administering the Lord's Supper.

The reasons of the doctrine are:

(1) There is no certain knowledge who has sanctifying grace. If we should be limited by God so that we might admit none to church fellowship but such as have sanctifying grace, we should be under extreme difficulties and great scruples of conscience; for if we make the most exact search, we should often be very much mistaken and in danger to accept some who were not sincere and to reject some who were sincere. There is no certain rule given in the Scripture to the guides of the church whereby they can distinguish saints from hypocrites. Neither do many persons know what to make of themselves. Some who are godly have many fears whether their hearts are right in the sight of God, which is implied in that precept, 2 Peter 1:10, *Give all diligence to make your calling and election sure*. And many hypocrites have a great deal of confidence that they are saints, John 9:40, *Are we blind also?*

It is not to be imagined that God would give a rule to His people that is impracticable. If that were the rule, that only godly men were to be admitted to communion in the church, there is not knowledge enough upon earth in order to the practice of it. The church, through their ignorance, must wholly forbear acting, for their knowledge of other men's piety is but a supposition, 1 Peter 5:12, *By Silvanus, a faithful brother as I suppose.* And particular persons would never be able to attend that rule for lack of the knowledge of themselves. Some would exclude themselves, and others would obtrude themselves contrary to it so that the rule would come to nothing. God's rules are such that no man has any just cause to object against them; but if this were the rule, that godly men only might enjoy ordinances, the church might object that it is God's prerogative to know the hearts of men, and we are utterly incapable of attending that rule.

(2) It is needful that others should attend duties of worship that the worship of God might be carried on. In the flourishing times of the church, that will hold, Matthew 20:16, *Many are called and few are chosen;* but there are degenerate times when religion runs very low among the people of God and, at such a time, there is a great scarcity of godly men. Psalm 12:1, *The godly man ceases, the faithful fail from among the children of men.* Isaiah 53:1, *Who hath believed our report, and to whom is the arm of the Lord revealed.* It may be that there may be only two or three sometimes in a parish. In some countries, especially godly men are very thinly sown, and if the rest must be excluded from any part of the worship of God, how can it be carried on, how can they show forth the Lord's death until He comes? Yes, if none but holy men must officiate in the church, they would be necessitated many times to be destitute of ministers. In some countries especially, it would be a difficult thing to find men qualified with sanctifying grace. Sometimes there is a great scarcity of godly magistrates, Jeremiah 5:1, *Run to and fro through the streets of Jerusalem, and see now and know and seek in the broad places thereof, if ye can find a man, if there be any that executeth judgment, that seeketh the truth, and I will pardon it.* So many times there is a great scarcity of godly minis-

ters, Matthew 23:3, *Do not after their works, for they say and do not.*

(3) This is very useful that men may obtain sanctifying grace. If men do not have it now, yet it will be a wonderful mercy if they can obtain it before they die, and the attending duties of worship are very serviceable to that end. Thereby, they are in the way to be gained, Psalm 29:9, *In His temple doth every one speak of His glory.* It is a blessed thing to be waiting upon God, Proverbs 8:34, *Blessed is the man that heareth me, watching daily at my gates, waiting at the posts of my doors.* The giving of converting grace is not limited to any one ordinance. Prayer is very serviceable that way, Proverbs 2:3, *If thou criest after knowledge and liftest up thy voice for understanding.* So the hearing of the Word is very serviceable. The entrance of God's Word gives light. So the Sacraments are very useful for conversion. God teaches us in baptism that we are naturally polluted, and that we need to be cleansed by the blood of Christ. God, in the Lord's Supper, invites us to come to Christ, makes an affecting representation of His sufferings for our sins, testifies to the sufficiency of Christ, confirms the truth of the Covenant of Grace, and teaches us that the promise of salvation to those that believe in Christ is certain. All sacraments are seals of the covenant, as circumcision was, Romans 4:11.

(4) The attending of those duties is part of the external covenant. The covenant people of God are bound to attend covenant duties. If any part of the external covenant is neglected, the covenant is broken. The covenant that God makes with His visible people ought to be attended. The visible people of God have a natural power to attend those duties, and they have a legal power to attend them; they may attend them lawfully. There is no part of the external covenant but it may be kept by the visible church. Therefore, they have power to qualify themselves sufficiently in order to the attending of them; but if sanctifying

grace were necessary in order to the lawful attending of them, then it would be out of their power.

The use of this doctrine is of warning. Do not be afraid to attend the duties of worship because you are destitute of sanctifying grace. Men who are destitute of sanctifying grace can perform no duty in an acceptable manner; but yet you must not give way to a spirit of fear so as to neglect your duty. Men must be afraid to neglect it and not afraid to attend it. You must make hast to get sanctifying grace, but you must not deny God any part of His worship until that is done. It is a poor thing for men to be scared into religion, but it is sad indeed for men to be scared out of religion and to neglect God's worship out of fear of God.

There are two things that make men neglect the Lord's Supper.

1. Some despise it. They don't find any need of it; their design is the world and their pleasures, and they don't regard the Lord's Supper. There is a profane spirit prevailing in the land; and many men neglect the Lord's Supper from the same reason that they neglect secret prayer, viz., because they despise holy things. They don't regard communion with God, nor helps and advantages to eternal life. They are far from that spirit David had who said, *One thing have I desired, and that I will seek after, that I may dwell in the house of the Lord all the days of my life, to behold the beauty of the Lord, and to inquire in His temple.*

2. Some are afraid of it. They are desirous to do anything they can for the promotion of their salvation; but they are afraid to attend that ordinance. It is with them as it was with David, 2 Samuel 6:9, *And David was afraid of the Lord that day, and said, How shall the ark of the Lord come to me?* They have drunk in an opinion that none but converted persons should come to that ordinance and so they neglect it. They have been misinformed about it and so dare not come; but they should not be afraid to attend that ordinance. Consider:

(1) Those who discourage persons from coming to it, because unconverted, in their zeal make others to cease from fearing the Lord. As the Reubenites and Gadites argued in somewhat alike case, Joshua 22:23-24. The neglecting of outward worship is the way to neglect inward worship. Staying away from ordinances is not the way to fit men for ordinances. The neglecting of the sacrament is the way to make the country grow profane. God's ordinances are the means to advance religion. If they neglect prayer, it would hinder them from fearing the Lord. If they neglect hearing the Word, if they neglect baptism, so likewise if they neglect the Lord's Supper, it will prove no advantage to religion to neglect any of God's ordinances. The solemn attending of God's ordinances leads men into a sense of the need of Christ and the benefit of Christ. The limiting of the Lord's Supper to a small number has a tendency to nourish carnal confidence in those who are admitted, and to nourish profaneness in those who are excluded.

(2) There can be no sufficient reason assigned why those who are destitute of sanctifying grace should be barred from the Lord's Supper. The holiness of the ordinance can be no reason, for circumcision and the Passover were holy ordinances, yet many unregenerate persons partook of them. Baptism is a holy ordinance, yet it may be administered to unregenerate men. The signification of the Lord's Supper can be no reason; it signifies Christ as suffering for our sins. The bread is the sign of His body and the wine is the sign of His blood. So the water in baptism is a sign of the blood of Christ, yet may be applied to unregenerate persons. The sign of Christ crucified is of great use to put them in mind of Christ's sufferings for us. Its being a seal of the covenant is no reason. It is of great use to them to see God sealing His covenant. As it is of use for God to declare His covenant, so to see God sealing His covenant. The testimony that is given to Christ in this ordinance can be no reason. It is very fit that they, as well as

others, should show forth His death.

(3) Many who judge that persons should be converted before they come to the Sacrament run into a great fault. They persuade persons that they are converted before they are. They are zealous against men's coming to the Lord's Supper in an unconverted condition, yet advise and encourage such persons to come under a notion that they are converted. If persons carry themselves civilly and religiously, they think they are converted, and urge them to join the church. Hereby, an abundance of wrong is done. Men are greatly hardened in a natural estate, and they are laid under great temptation to flatter themselves as if the bitterness of death was past. This is a means to prevent many men's conversions. If men are made to believe that they are godly before they are, that is likely to prove a mighty impediment unto their conversion. They don't lie open to the threatenings of the Word. They think others are spoken to and they pity them; but they are not sensible of their own danger, John 9:41, *Because you say you see, therefore your sin remaineth.*

(4) If none who are destitute of sanctifying grace may come, then two sorts of persons who do come should stay away. First, such persons as are in a natural condition, yet have confidence that they are converted. There are many such persons, Proverbs 30:12, *There is a generation that are pure in their own eyes, yet are not cleansed from their filthiness.* But there is no way to keep them from it. The church can't keep them from it, because they are visible saints, and their own consciences will not forbid, because they are confident that they are converted.

And secondly, there is another sort that should forbear: such godly men as do not know that they are converted. If a man is godly, yet how can he, with a good conscience, come to an ordinance peculiar to godly men, when he doesn't know himself to be godly? If only saints are allowed to come, he must know himself to be a saint before he can know that he is allowed by God to come. As if a man has power to sell nothing but what is his own, then he must know a thing to be his own before he can sell it with a good conscience. Or if a church has power to censure only scandalous persons, then they must know a man to be scandalous before they can, with a good conscience, censure him. So, in this case, if the Sacrament is only for godly men, they don't know that they have any right to it until they know they are godly.

(5) It is from the misunderstanding of one Scripture principally that these are afraid to come to the Lord's Supper, viz., 1 Corinthians 11. There are two expressions in that chapter that terrify them. One is that *he that eateth and drinketh unworthily is guilty of the body and blood of the Lord,* that is, of profaning the ordinance. And they are said to *eat and drink damnation or judgment to themselves.* But this unworthy eating is doing of it in a rude manner, as verse 21, *For in eating everyone taketh before others his own supper, and one is hungry and another is drunken.* And he explains himself, verse 29, *not discerning the Lord's body,* that is, not discerning that bread from common bread. Another expression is, *Let a man examine himself and so let him eat,* verse 28. But it is not said, "Let him examine himself whether he should eat or forbear," but *let him examine himself and so let him eat.* The meaning is that he must come solemnly to that ordinance, examining what need he has of it.

(6) The church is bound to receive men if they are externally qualified, whether they are godly or not. If men make a profession and are not scandalous in their conversation, the church cannot refuse them. The Apostle still received those who made a profession of the gospel, Acts 2:41 and 6:7. Those who are saints by calling are to be accepted by the church whether they are converted or not. The matter of the church is visible saints. If the church were only to receive those who were converted, God would

have given them a certain rule in attending as to which unconverted persons should be excluded, but there is no such rule given. Neither is there any external sign that certainly distinguishes converted men from unconverted. The church is not concerned to see that they are all real saints, their work is to see that they are visible saints. If they reject such, they are to blame.

(7) It cannot be an unlawful thing for men to keep the external covenant. As the visible people of God have a natural power, so they have a lawful power to keep the external covenant. If they keep the external covenant, they are accepted as a righteous people, Deuteronomy 6:25, *It shall be our righteousness if we observe to do all these commandments.* If they neglect to do any part of the covenant, they lay themselves open to the judgments of God. God brings war to avenge the quarrel of His covenant, and this is one part of God's covenant, Genesis 17:10. Circumcision is called the covenant. So this is one branch of the covenant. It is required in the second command that we worship God in that way which He has appointed; and this is the appointment of God, that His whole visible church celebrate the memorial of the death of Christ, 1 Corinthians 10:17, *We being many do all partake of that one bread.* And indeed, it is the duty of the church to require all its adult orderly members to come to the Lord's Supper, and it would be very strange that it should be the duty of the church to require them to come, and censure them for not coming, and yet be their duty to stay away because unconverted.

(8) It is exceedingly strange that it should be the institution of God that only converted persons should come to the Lord's Supper, and yet no more care taken that this institution should be attended. If it were God's will that no unconverted person should come, it is much that He does not charge His church to use their utmost endeavors to discover secret hypocrites and to keep them out of the church,

and that He doesn't command them to pluck up all the tares they can discover among the wheat as was proposed in Matthew 13:28. And is it not much that He does not charge unconverted men not to meddle with those holy things, and tell them that they must content themselves with praying and fasting, hearing and being baptized, but proceed no further? But we find no such injunctions in the Scripture.

(9) We have no cause to wonder to find some divines of our own nation, and some of other nations, to deny that the Supper is a converting ordinance. I find Wendiline, a great divine in his disputations against the Lutherans, acknowledging again and again that the sacraments may instrumentally begin faith in adult persons and, in another place, saying that the sacraments of confirmation (he means Passover and the Lord's Supper) may organically begin faith. Yet there are a great many divines that deny this. But this is not to be wondered at, seeing they hold that elect infants who have federal holiness have, at the same time, the internal grace of regeneration. And he says that Dr. Burgess proves by many divines that elect infants have an initial and seminal regeneration upon their baptism. If it were so, no doubt but their actual conversion would be in early days before they come to that age when persons are wont to be admitted to the Lord's Supper.

(10) No Christian country neglects this ordinance as we do in this land. In our own nation at home, so in Scotland, Holland, Denmark, Sweden and among the Protestants in Germany and France, they generally celebrate the memorial of Christ's death. This country is singular in neglecting it. About forty years past, there was a multitude in this country unbaptized, but that neglect was taken into examination, and now there is an alteration in that particular. But to this day there are four to one who neglect the Lord's Supper, as if it did not belong to them to magnify God upon the account of the work of redemption. We are a people who pretend high in religion, but indeed

we fall short of other people in the very form of it, and don't come up in our practice in this particular to many other churches.

(11) The general neglect of this ordinance is a visible denying of the gospel. Christ has threatened to deny them before His Father who deny Him before men, Matthew 10:33. And the neglect of this institution is a visible denial of Christ. Our business at the Lord's Supper is to celebrate the memorial of Christ's death and to give our testimony to the gospel, 1 Corinthians 11:26, *As often as ye eat this bread and drink this cup, ye show forth the Lord's death till He come.* They, therefore, who neglect to do this withhold their testimony. They act as if they did not believe the doctrine to be true. What construction can be put upon it but that they are unconcerned to give their testimony to Christ and question the truth of the gospel. It is an open reproaching of Christ and a visible contempt of the gospel. This neglect has a great tendency to strengthen and confirm others in their infidelity, for they act as if they did not believe it. And many children, when they are reproved for their infidelity, have that excuse for themselves, that their fathers and mothers do not believe the gospel.

(12) The neglect of this ordinance is one great cause of God's judgments. We are under sorrowful dispensations, and have reason to conclude this neglect to be one special cause of them. There is indeed an abundance of moral evils in the land which provoke God to anger, but generally, when God brought judgments upon Israel, it was mainly for corruptions in worship. As we may not introduce ceremonies of men's invention, so we must not neglect ordinances which are of divine institution. Neglects of worship bring destroying judgments, Exodus 5:3, *Let us sacrifice to the Lord our God, lest He fall upon us with pestilence or with sword.* Let men have what pretenses they will, yet those pretenses will not excuse them in the neglect of God's ordinances. God doesn't allow men to be scared out

of His worship. But I judge that the generality who do neglect it do so out of a careless and profane spirit, and then it is no wonder if it brings down the wrath of God.

OBJECTION. It is objected by some against this doctrine that if the Lord's Supper is a converting ordinance, then not only such as are civil and religious may be admitted to it, but profane and vicious persons, for they likewise need conversion, and it is a pity but they should have all helps to conversion.

ANSWER 1. Baptism is a converting ordinance, but yet it is not to be administered to adult persons who are profane, for baptism is only a converting ordinance to the members of the church who are unconverted. The hearing of the Word only is the appointed means for the conversion of others.

ANSWER 2. The Lord's Supper is an ordinance for the strengthening and exercising of grace, yet it does not follow that it is to be administered to godly men who are guilty of scandal. The need that they have to have their grace strengthened is no argument that the Lord's Supper should, in that case, be administered to them.

ANSWER 3. Though the Lord's Supper is a converting ordinance, yet it is not to be administered to any profane and vicious men, for it is a converting ordinance only to those who it is appointed to be administered unto, viz., members of the church walking orderly. When church members conduct themselves scandalously, there are other ordinances appointed for their conversion in case they are unconverted.

OBJECTION. It is also objected that those who were unclean were not to partake of the Passover, Numbers 9:7, which seems to hold forth to us that those who are spiritually unclean in the days of the gospel may not partake of the Lord's Supper.

ANSWER 1. If those who were spiritually unclean might come to the Passover, no reason can be assigned why they may not also come to the Lord's Supper, for the Passover was a holy ordinance as well as the Lord's Supper, and the Passover ought to be attended in a holy manner as well as the Supper.

ANSWER 2. The ordinances of the Old Testament were not types of the ordinances of the New Testament. If the reason why the unclean might not come to the Passover was to signify that those who were unregenerate might not come to the Lord's Supper, of what edification would that be to the Jews? They did not understand any such meaning and, if they had, it would have done them no good. But the ordinances of the Old Testament signified evangelical doctrines which were of great use to the Jews, so this appointment that unclean persons might not come to the Passover signified that those who were spiritually unclean should not have communion with God in the highest heaven, but be excluded out of the kingdom of God.

FINIS